For Engineers & Designers

CorelCAD Exercises

200 3D PRACTICE DRAWINGS

SACHIDANAND JHA

Dear Reader,

Thank you for choosing **CorelCAD Exercises** book. This book is part of a family of premium-quality CADIN360 books, all of which are written by Outstanding author who combine practical experience with a gift for teaching.

CADIN360 was founded in 2016. More than 3 years later, we're still committed to producing consistently exceptional books. With each of our titles, we're working hard to set a new standard for the industry. From the paper we print on, to the authors we work with, our goal is to bring you the best books available.

I hope you see all that reflected in these pages. I'd be very interested to hear your comments and get your feedback on how we're doing. Feel free to let me know what you think about this or any other CADIN360 book by sending me an email at contactus@cadin360.com.

If you think you've found a technical error in this book, please visit
https://cadin360.com/contact-us/.
Customer feedback is critical to our efforts at CADIN360.

Best regards,

Sachidanand Jha
Founder & CEO, CADIN360

CorelCAD Exercises

Published by
CADIN360
cadin360.com
Copyright © 2019 by CADIN360, All rights reserved.

Preface

CorelCAD Exercises

❖ This book contain 200 CAD practice exercises and drawings.

❖ This book does not provide step by step tutorial to design 3D models.

❖ S.I Unit is used.

❖ Predominantly used Third Angle Projection.

❖ This book is for **CorelCAD** and Other Feature-Based Modeling Software such as Inventor, SolidWorks, NX, Solid Edge, AutoCAD, PTC Creo etc.

❖ It is intended to provide Drafters, Designers and Engineers with enough 3D CAD exercises for practice on **CorelCAD**.

❖ It includes almost all types of exercises that are necessary to provide, clear, concise and systematic information required on industrial machine part drawings.

❖ Third Angle Projection is intentionally used to familiarize Drafters, Designers and Engineers in Third Angle Projection to meet the expectation of world wide Engineering drawing print.

❖ Clear and well drafted drawing help easy understanding of the design.

❖ This book is for Beginner, Intermediate and Advance CAD users.

❖ These exercises are from Basics to Advance level.

❖ Each exercises can be assigned and designed separately.

❖ No Exercise is a prerequisite for another. All dimensions are in mm.

❖ Note: Assume any missing dimensions.

EX-01

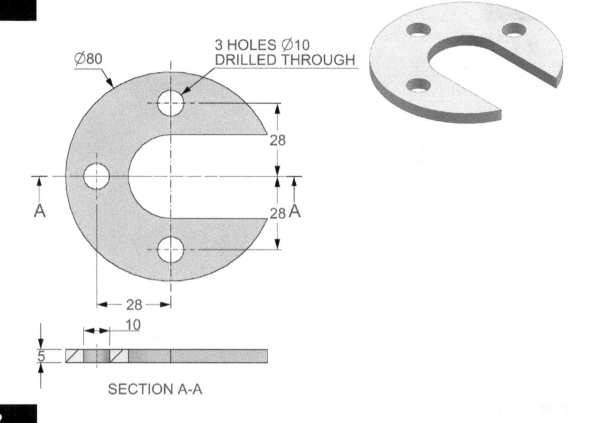

∅80

3 HOLES ∅10
DRILLED THROUGH

28

28 A

A

28

10

5

SECTION A-A

EX-02

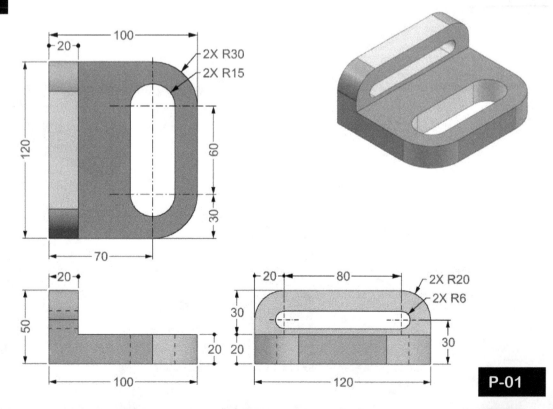

100

20

2X R30

2X R15

120

60

30

70

20

50

100

20

20

20

30

80

2X R20

2X R6

30

120

P-01

EX-03

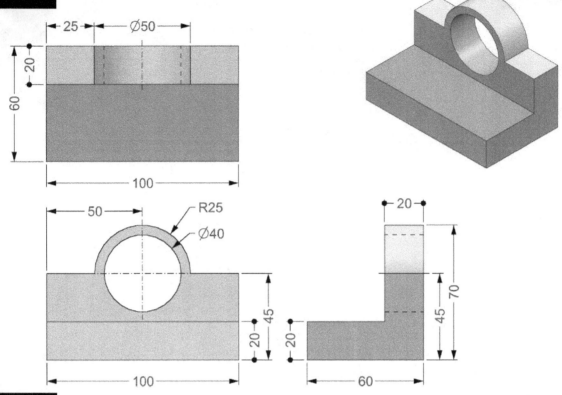

EX-04`

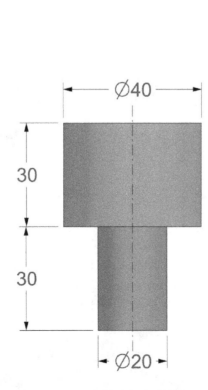

P-02

EX-05

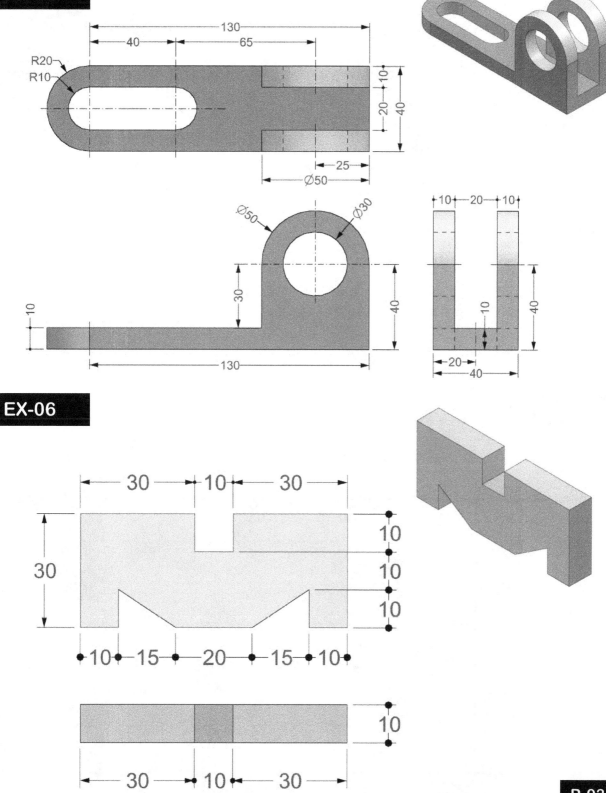

EX-06

P-03

EX-07

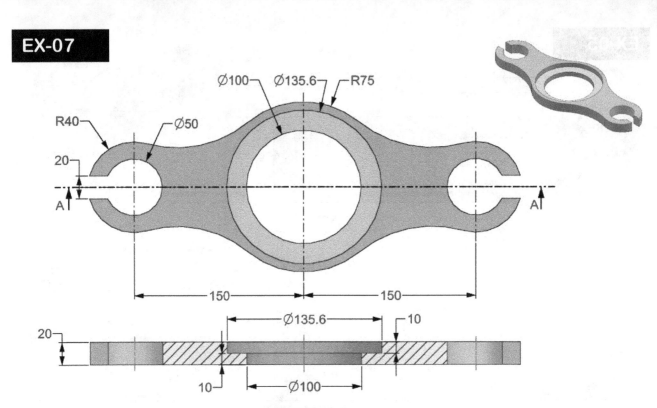

Ø100 Ø135.6 R75

R40 Ø50

20

A

A

150 150

Ø135.6 10

20

10 Ø100

SECTION A-A
(SCALE 1:1)

EX-08

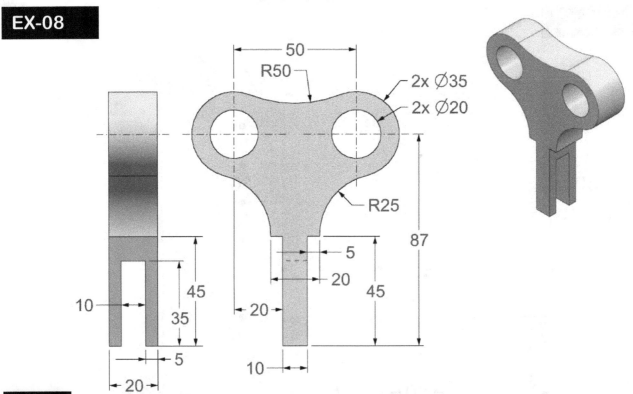

50

R50

2x Ø35

2x Ø20

R25

87

5

20

45

45

10 20

10

35

20

5

20

EX-09

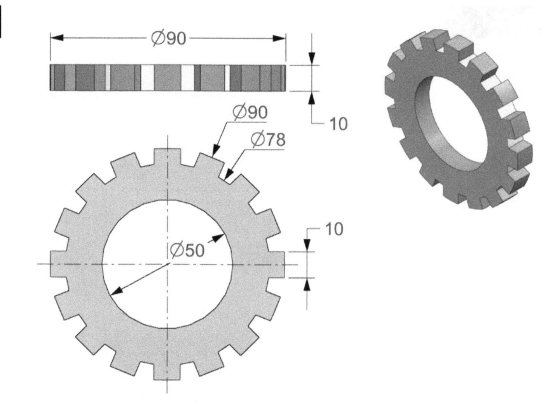

⌀90

10

⌀90
⌀78
⌀50

10

EX-10

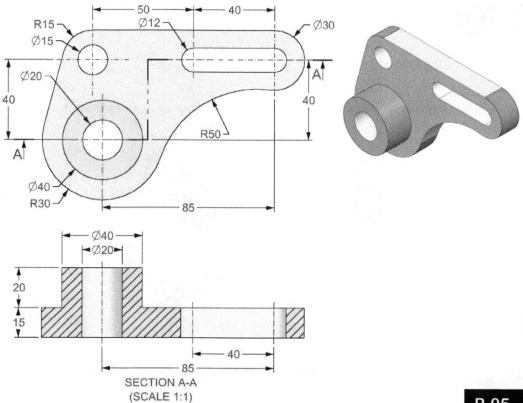

R15
⌀15
⌀20
40
A
⌀40
R30

50
⌀12

40
⌀30

A
40

R50

85

⌀40
⌀20

20

15

40

85

SECTION A-A
(SCALE 1:1)

P-05

EX-11

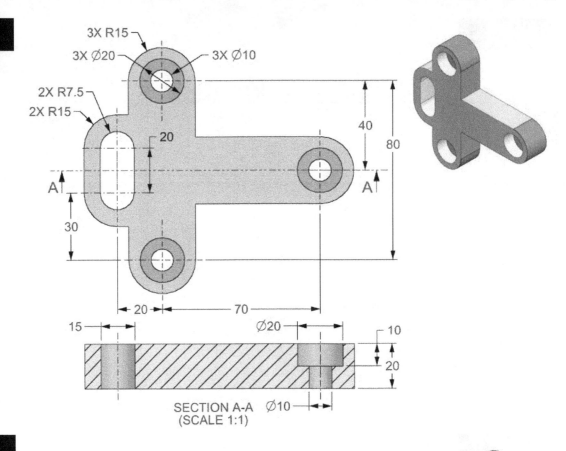

3X R15
3X Ø20
3X Ø10
2X R7.5
2X R15
20
40
80
A
30
A
20
70
15
Ø20
10
20

SECTION A-A
(SCALE 1:1)
Ø10

EX-12

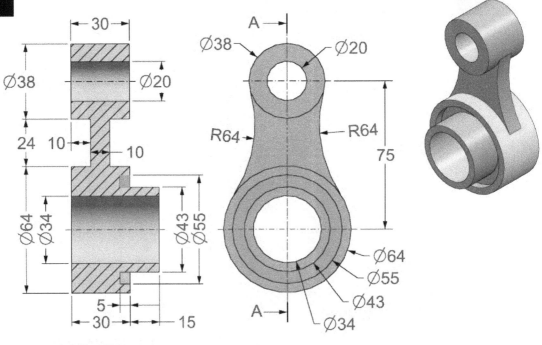

30
Ø38
Ø20
24   10
10
Ø64
Ø34
Ø43
Ø55
5
30
15

A
Ø38
Ø20
R64
R64
75
Ø64
Ø55
Ø43
Ø34
A

SECTION A-A
(SCALE 1:1)

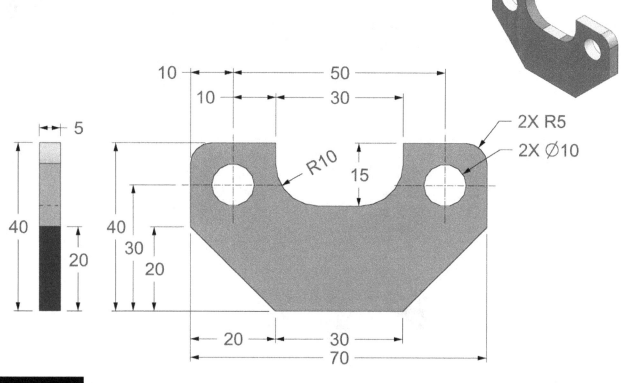

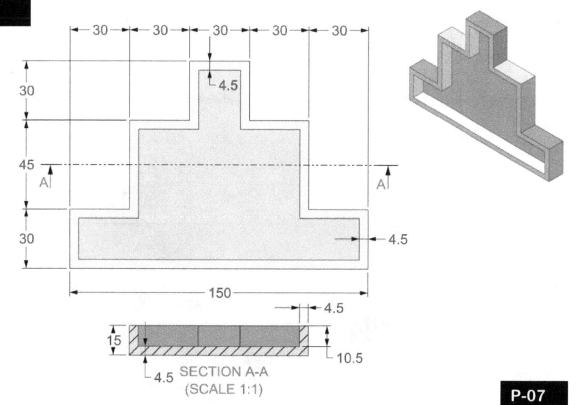

SECTION A-A
(SCALE 1:1)

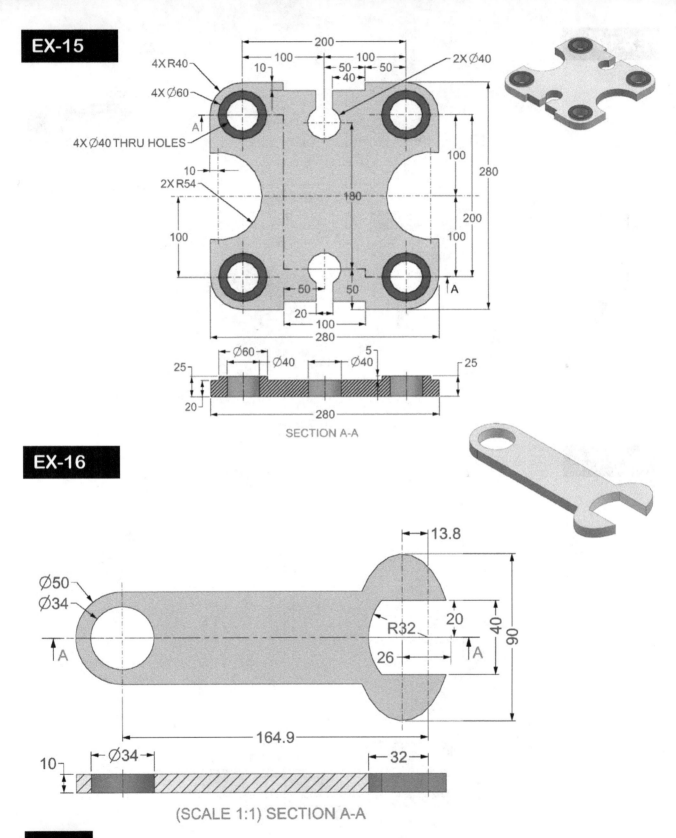

EX-15

4X R40
4X Ø60
4X Ø40 THRU HOLES
2X R54

200
100
100
10
50
50
40
2X Ø40

100
280
180
200
100

10
100

50
50
20
100
280

SECTION A-A

Ø60
Ø40
Ø40
5
25
25
20
280

EX-16

Ø50
Ø34
13.8
R32
20
40
90
26

A
A
164.9

Ø34
32
10

(SCALE 1:1) SECTION A-A

P-08

EX-17

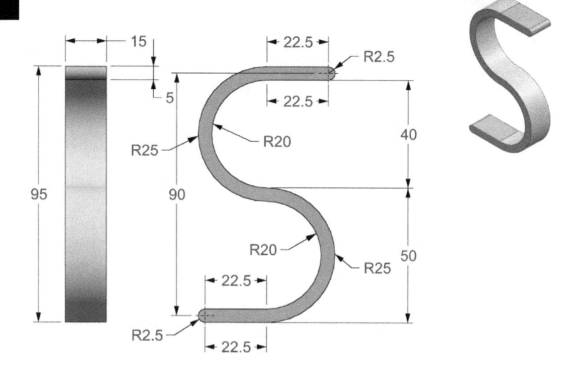

15
95
5
22.5
22.5
R2.5
R20
R25
40
90
R20
R25
50
22.5
R2.5
22.5

EX-18

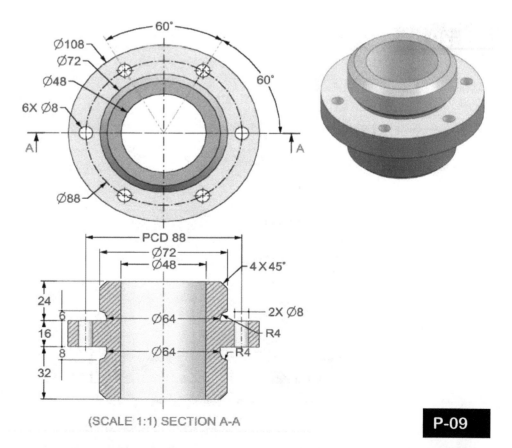

Ø108
Ø72
Ø48
6X Ø8
60°
60°
Ø88

PCD 88
Ø72
Ø48
4 X 45°
24
6
Ø64
2X Ø8
R4
16
8
Ø64
R4
32

(SCALE 1:1) SECTION A-A

P-09

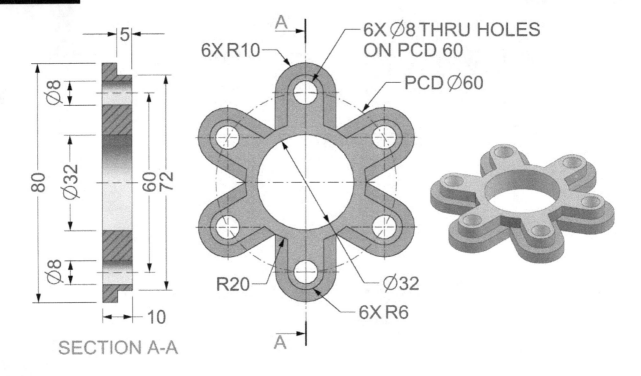

6X R10

6X Ø8 THRU HOLES
ON PCD 60

PCD Ø60

Ø8

Ø32

80

60

72

Ø8

R20

Ø32

6X R6

10

5

SECTION A-A

A

A

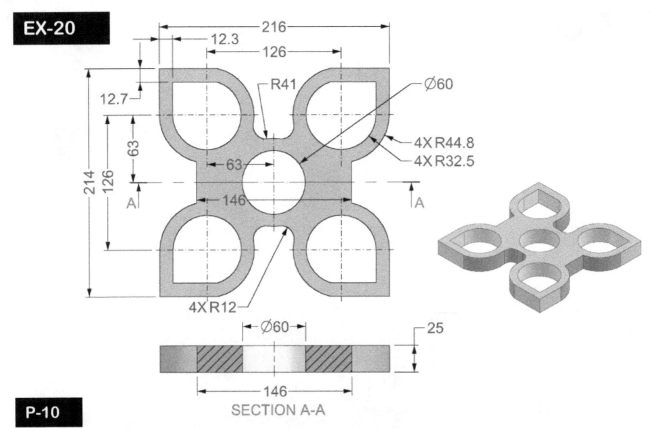

216

12.3

126

R41

Ø60

12.7

63

4X R44.8
4X R32.5

63

214

126

A

A

146

4X R12

Ø60

25

146

SECTION A-A

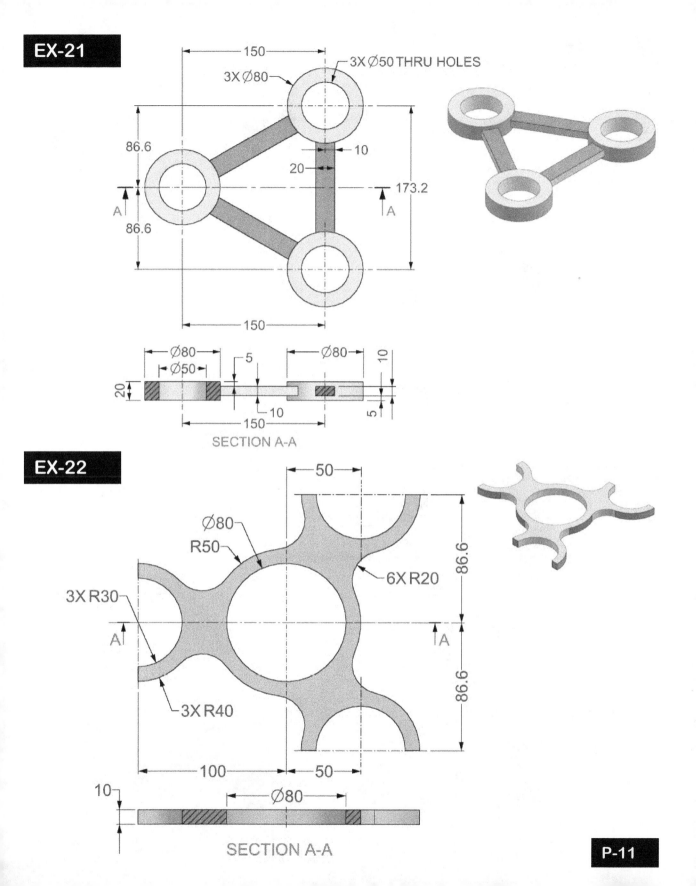

EX-21

150
3X Ø80
3X Ø50 THRU HOLES
86.6
10
20
173.2
A
A
86.6
150

Ø80
Ø50
5
Ø80
10
20
10
5
150
SECTION A-A

EX-22

50
Ø80
R50
86.6
6X R20
3X R30
A
A
3X R40
86.6
100
50

10
Ø80
SECTION A-A

P-11

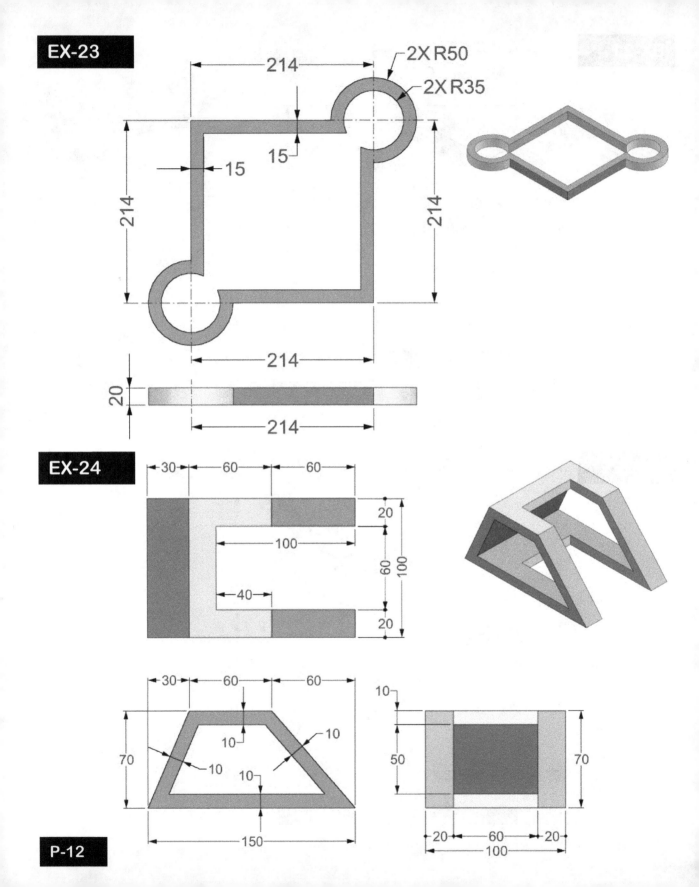

EX-23

214

2X R50

2X R35

15

15

214

214

214

214

20

214

EX-24

30 · 60 · 60

20

100

60 100

40

20

30 · 60 · 60

10

10

70

10

10

10

150

10

50

70

20 · 60 · 20

100

P-12

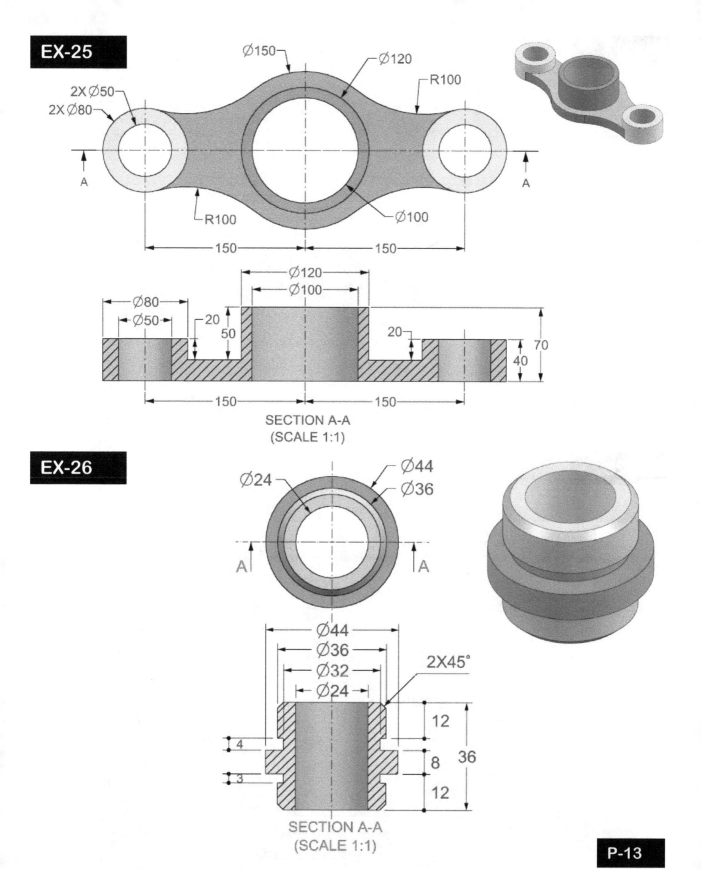

EX-25

∅150
∅120
R100
2X ∅50
2X ∅80
∅100
R100
150
150

∅120
∅100
∅80
∅50
20
50
20
70
40
150
150

SECTION A-A
(SCALE 1:1)

EX-26

∅24
∅44
∅36

∅44
∅36
∅32
∅24
2X45°
12
8
36
12
4
3

SECTION A-A
(SCALE 1:1)

P-13

EX-27

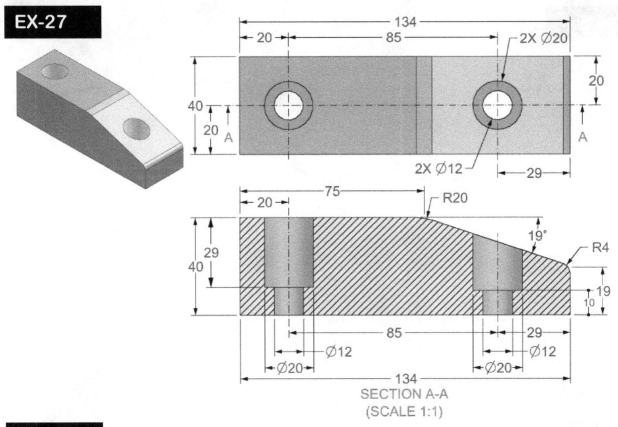

134
20
85
2X Ø20
40
20
20
A
A
2X Ø12
29

20
75
R20
29
40
19°
R4
85
29
19
10
Ø12
Ø12
Ø20
Ø20
134
SECTION A-A
(SCALE 1:1)

EX-28

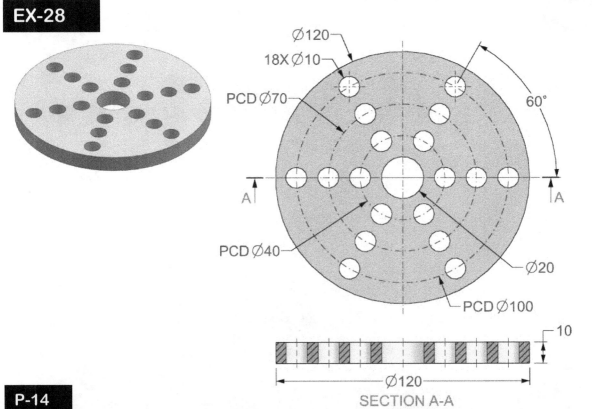

Ø120
18X Ø10
PCD Ø70
60°
PCD Ø40
Ø20
PCD Ø100
A
A

10
Ø120
SECTION A-A

EX-29

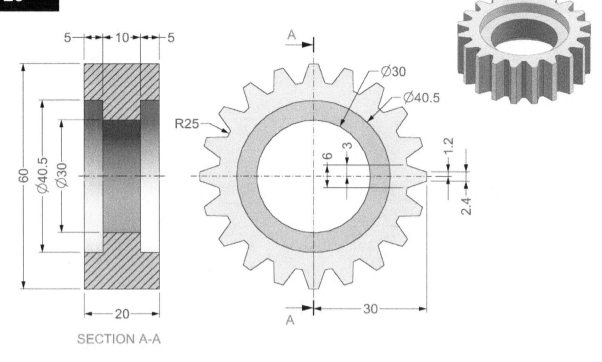

SECTION A-A

EX-30

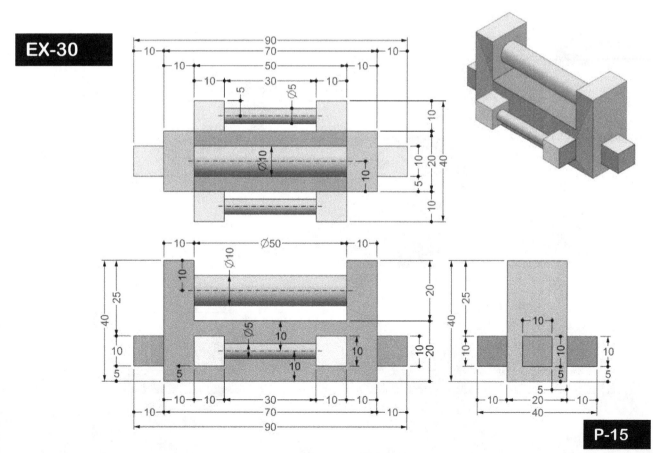

P-15

EX-31

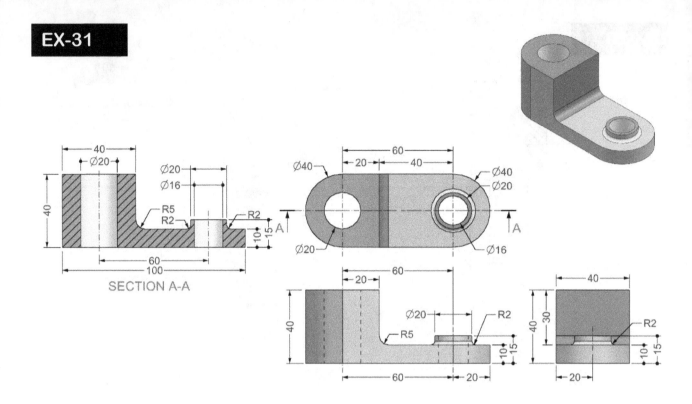

SECTION A-A

EX-32

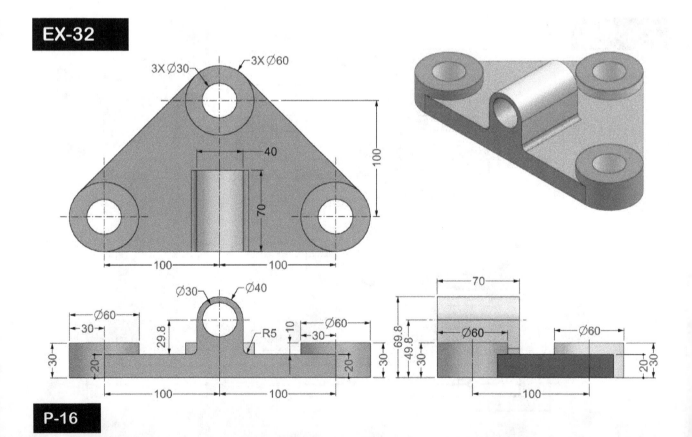

P-16

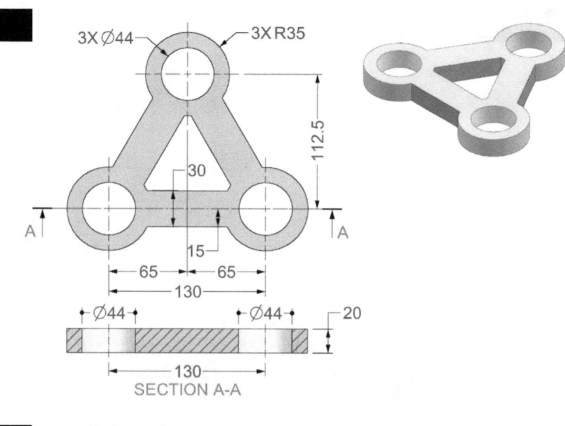

3X Ø44 — 3X R35

112.5

30

15

65 65

130

Ø44 Ø44 20

130

SECTION A-A

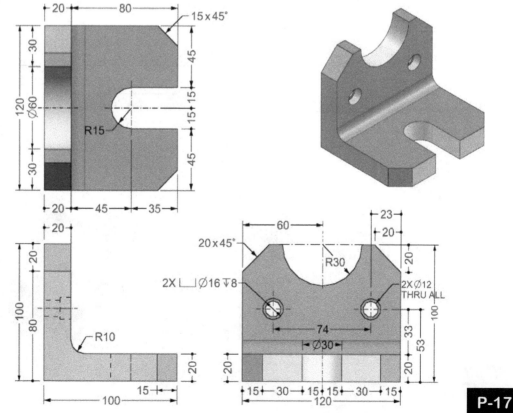

20 80 15 x 45°

30

45

120 Ø60 15 15

15

R15

30 45

20 45 35

20

20

100

80

R10

15

100

20 x 45°

60 23

20

R30

2X ⌴ Ø16 ▼8

2X Ø12 THRU ALL

20

74

100

Ø30

33

53

20

15 30 15 15 30 15

120

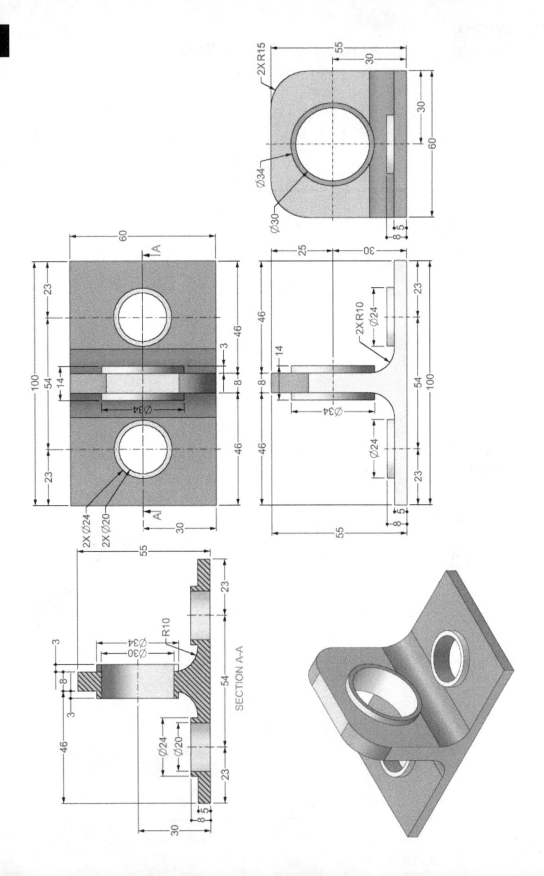

SECTION A-A

2X R15
55
30
30
60
Ø34
Ø30
8
5

60
A
23
100
54
14
Ø34
23
2X Ø24
2X Ø20
A
30
3
46
8
46

25
30
46
14
8
2X R10
Ø24
23
54
100
Ø34
Ø24
23
8
5
55

2X Ø24
2X Ø20
55
3
8
3
46
R10
Ø34
Ø30
Ø24
Ø20
23
54
23
8
5
30

EX-36

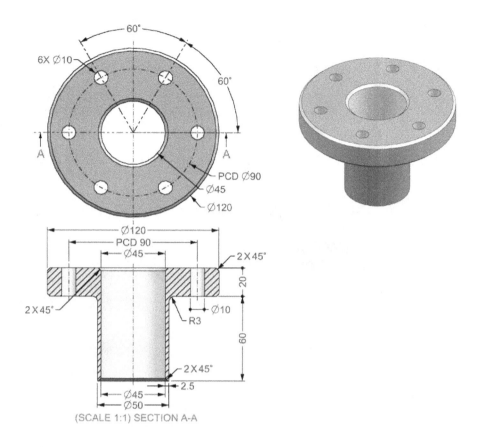

60°

6X Ø10

60°

PCD Ø90
Ø45
Ø120

Ø120
PCD 90
Ø45

2 X 45°
20

2 X 45°
Ø10
R3

60

2 X 45°
2.5
Ø45
Ø50

(SCALE 1:1) SECTION A-A

A   A

EX-37

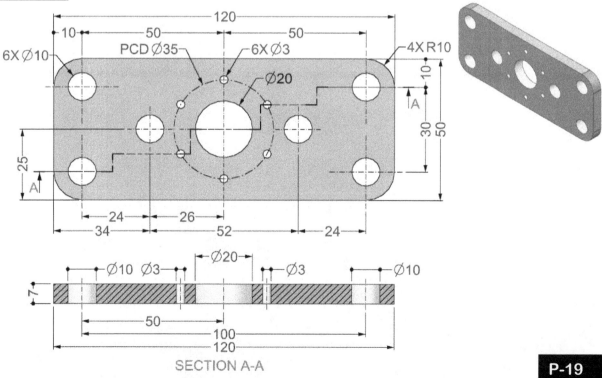

120

10   50   50

6X Ø10   PCD Ø35   6X Ø3   4X R10

Ø20

10

A

30   50

25

A

24   26

34   52   24

Ø20

Ø10 Ø3   Ø3   Ø10

7

50

100

120

SECTION A-A

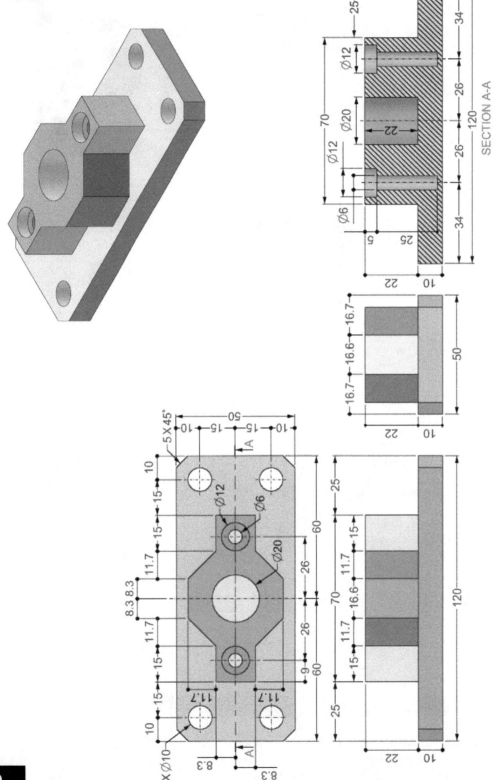

SECTION A-A

EX-39

R20
Ø20

70

40

45

45

R25
Ø20

20

30

10

10

A

A

45

65

2X R10
Ø40
Ø20

20

25

45

SECTION A-A

EX-40

Ø60

20

10

5

Ø50

Ø60
Ø50

5   10   5

30

Ø60

20

P-21

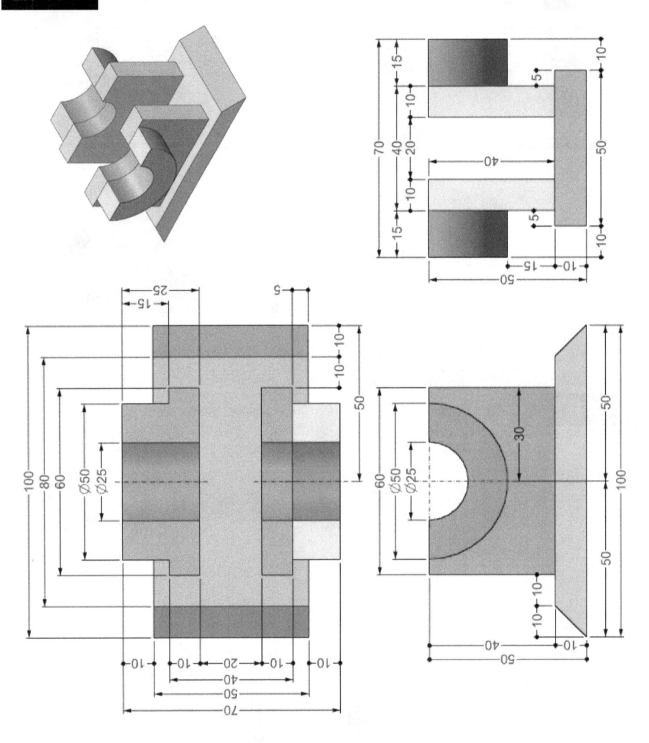

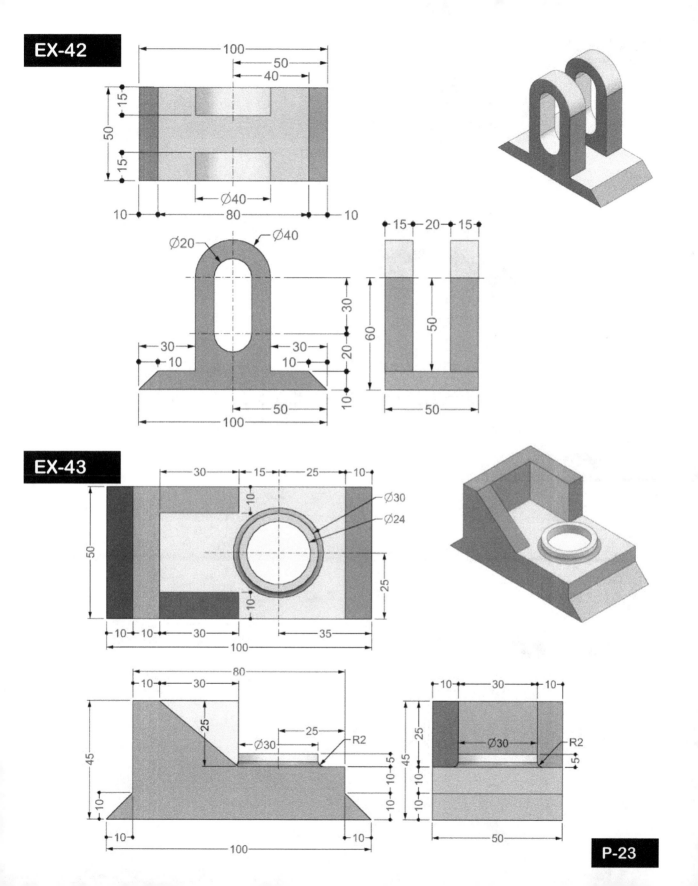

EX-42

EX-43

P-23

EX-44

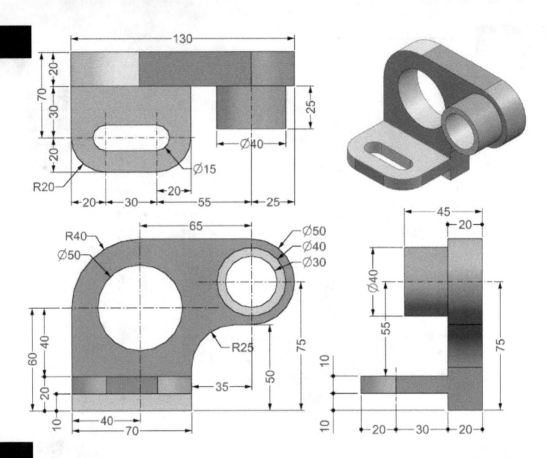

EX-45

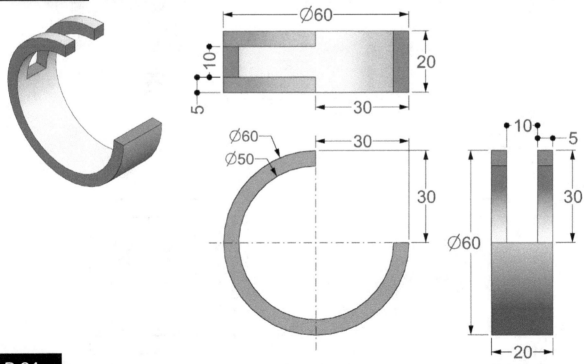

EX-46

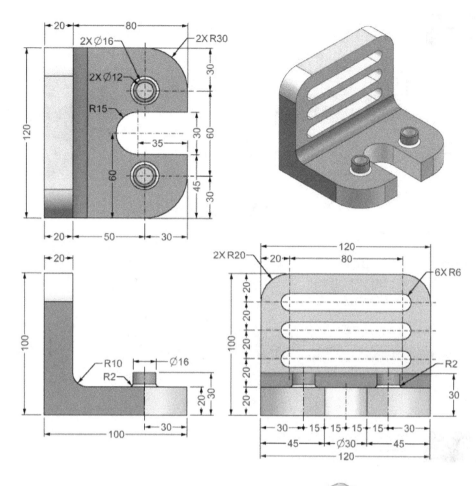

EX-47

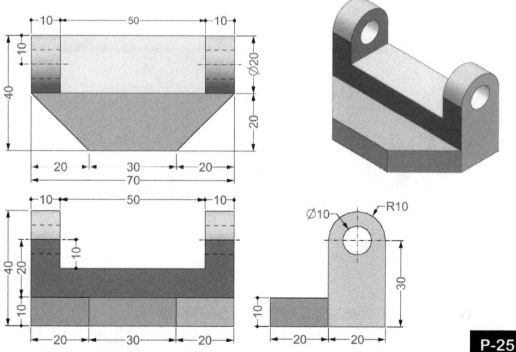

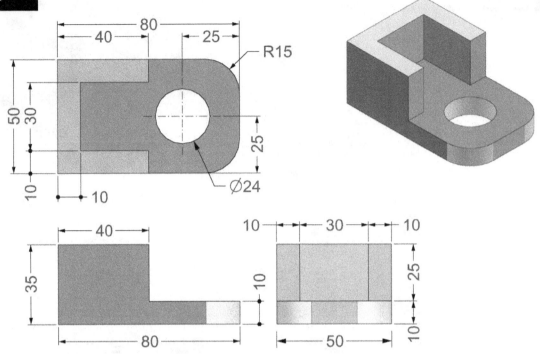

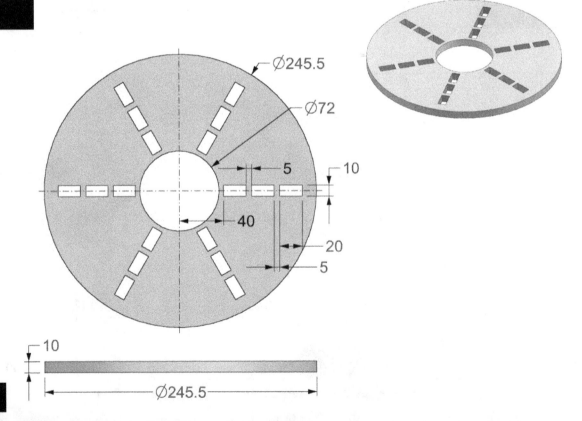

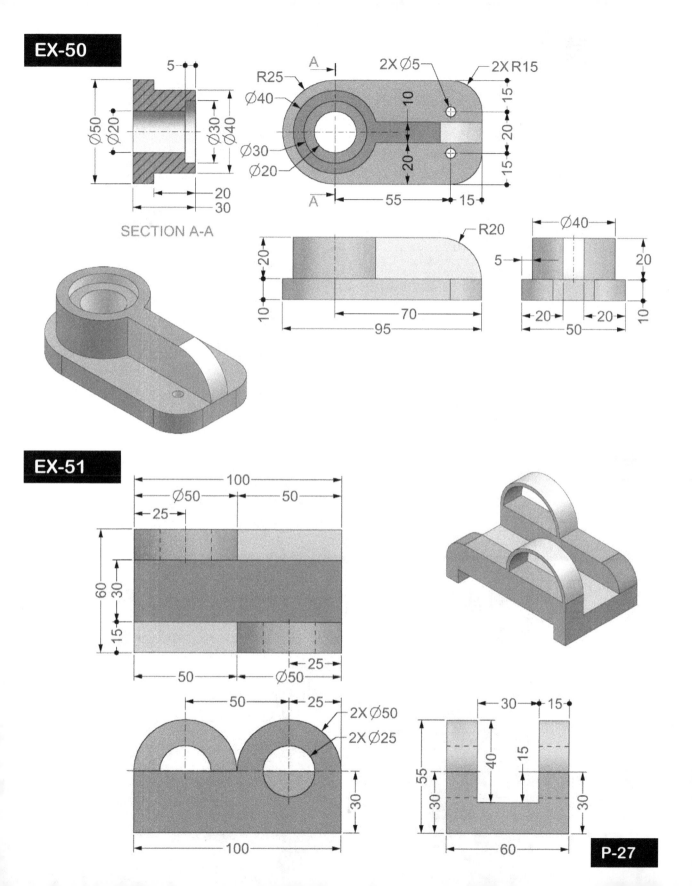

EX-50

5
⌀50
⌀20
⌀30
⌀40
20
30

SECTION A-A

A
R25
⌀40
⌀30
⌀20
2X ⌀5
2X R15
10
15
20
15
20
15
55
15
A

R20
20
10
70
95

⌀40
5
20
20
50
20
10

EX-51

100
⌀50
50
25
60
30
15
50
25
⌀50

50
25
2X ⌀50
2X ⌀25
30
100

30
15
55
40
15
30
30
60

P-27

EX-52

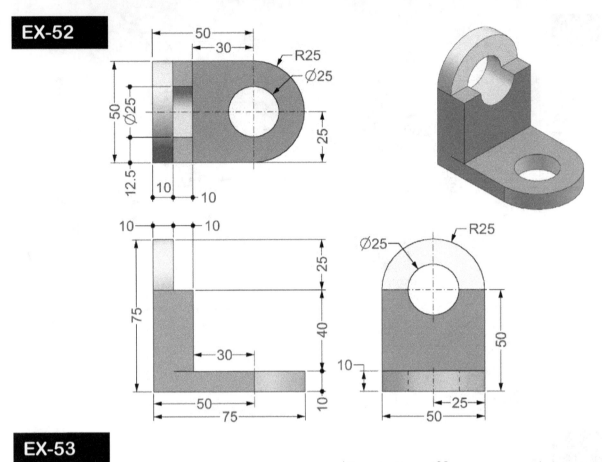

EX-53

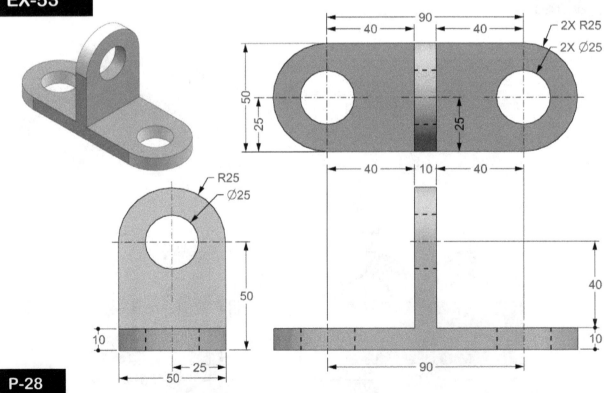

P-28

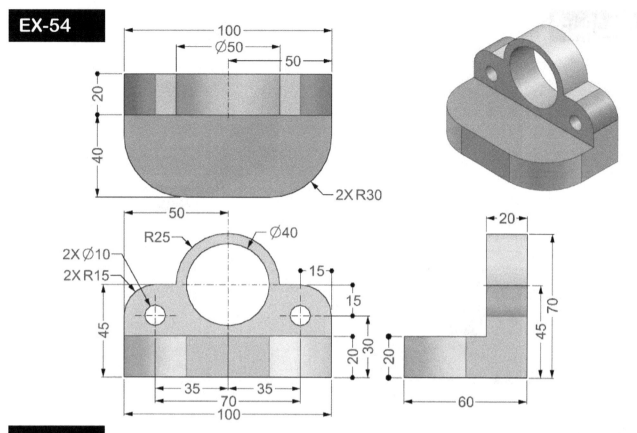

100
Ø50
50
20
40
2X R30

50
R25
Ø40
2X Ø10
2X R15
15
15
45
20
30
20
35
35
70
100
20
70
45
60

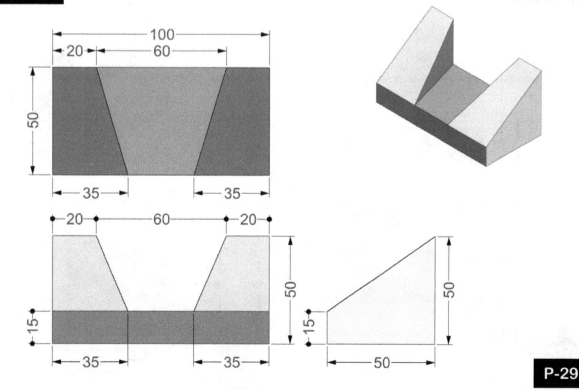

100
20
60
50
35
35
20
60
20
50
15
35
35
15
50
50

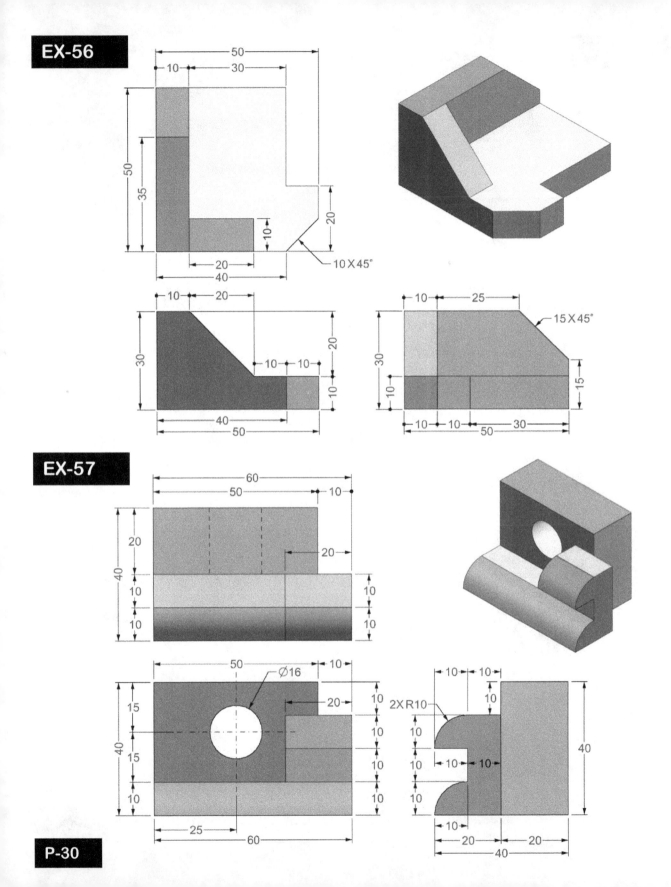

EX-56

EX-57

P-30

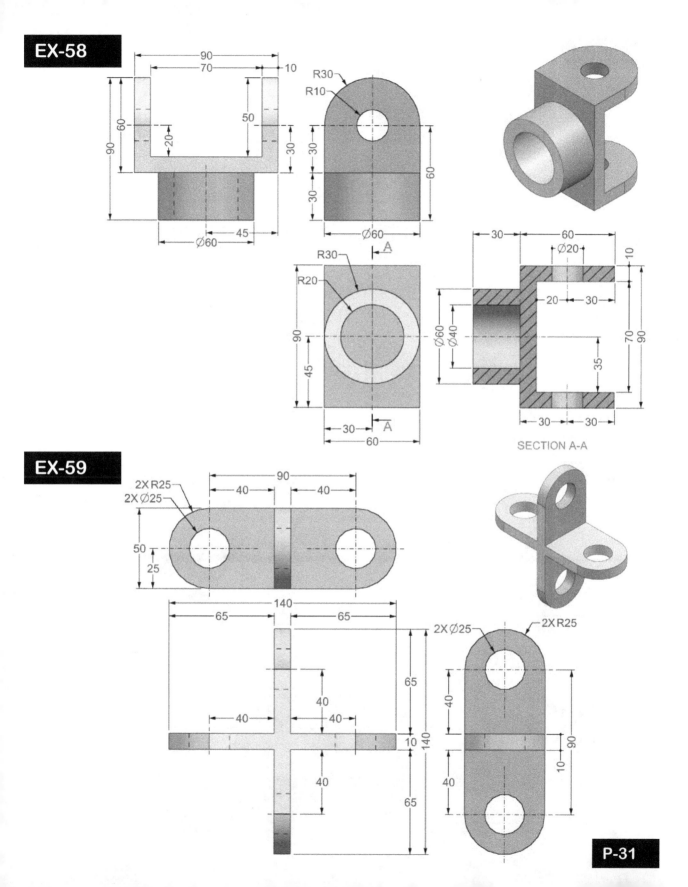

EX-58

90
70
10
90
60
50
20
30
45
Ø60

R30
R10
30
30
60
Ø60

A

R30
R20
90
45
30
60

A

30
60
Ø20
10
Ø60
Ø40
20
30
70
90
35
30
30

SECTION A-A

EX-59

2X R25
2X Ø25
90
40
40
50
25

140
65
65
65
140
40
40
40
10
65
40

2X Ø25
2X R25
40
90
10
40

P-31

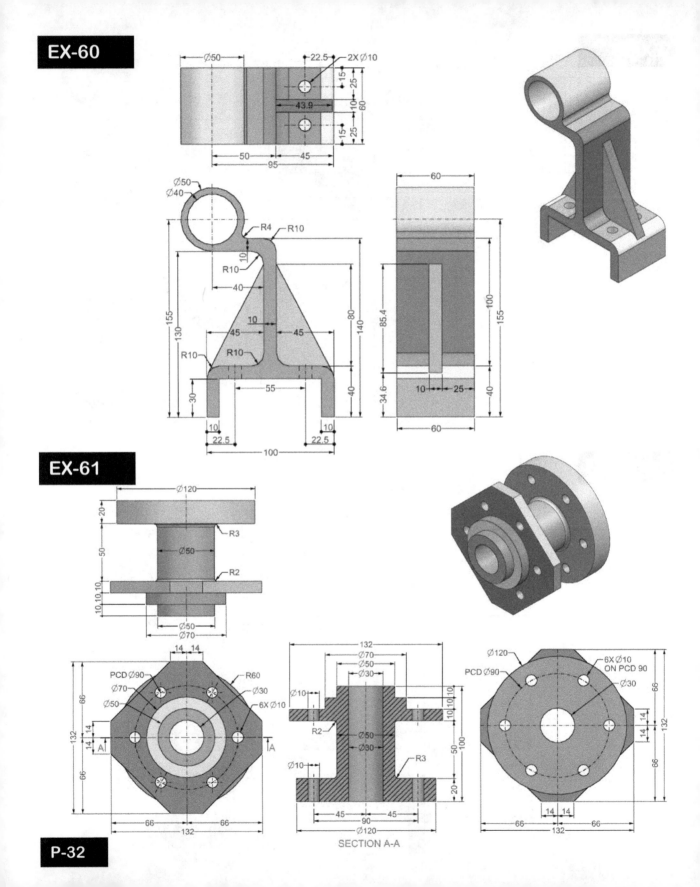

EX-60

EX-61

P-32

SECTION A-A

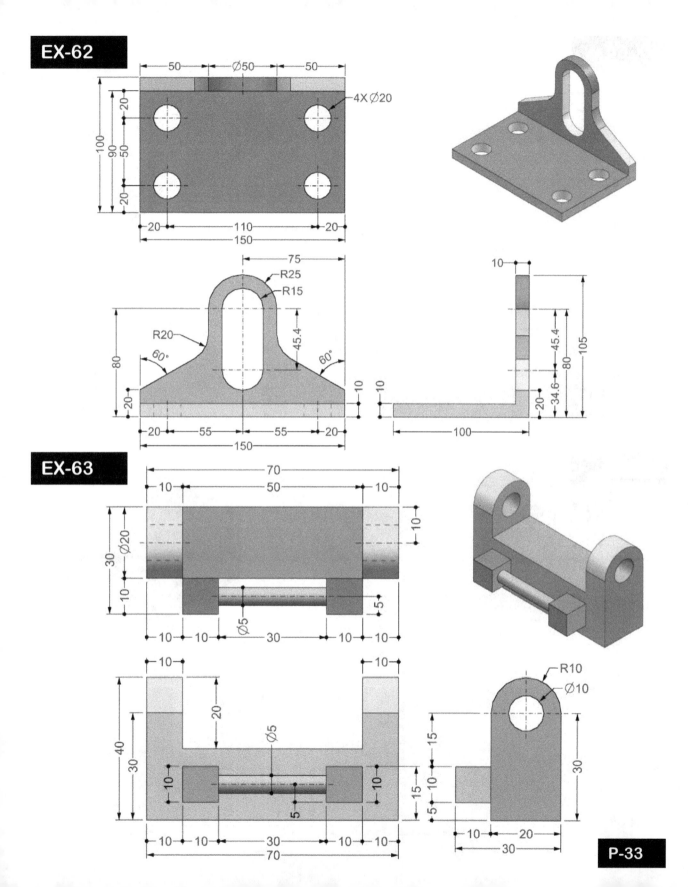

EX-62

4X⌀20

EX-63

P-33

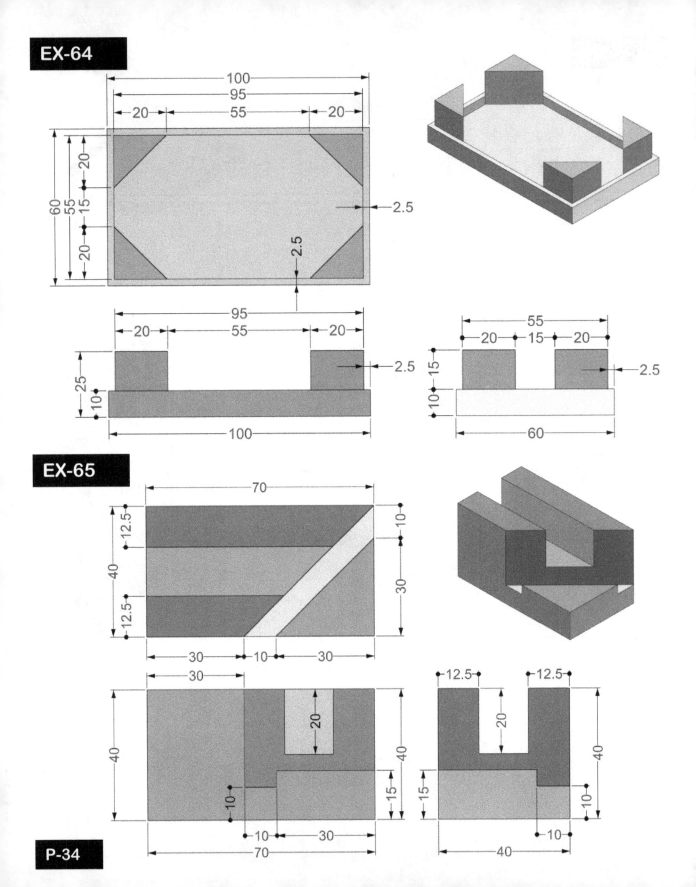

EX-64

EX-65

P-34

EX-66

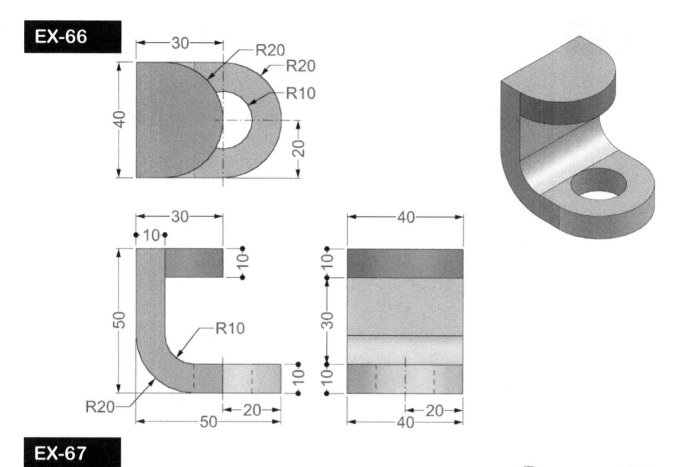

EX-67

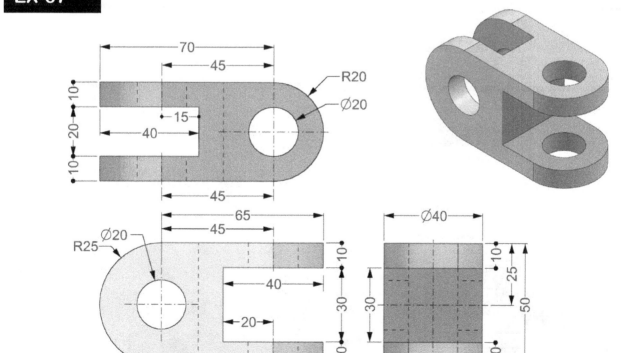

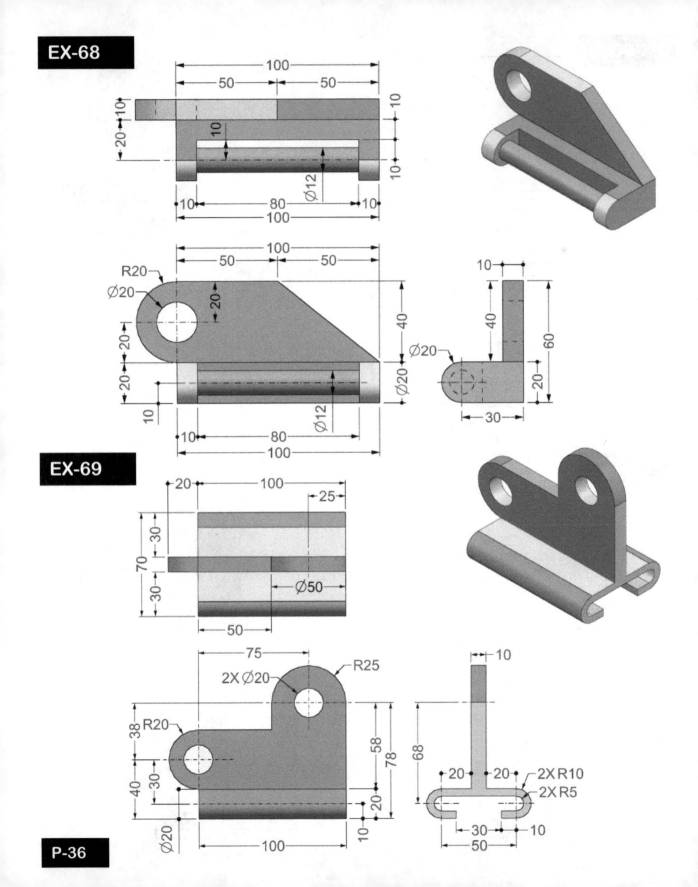

EX-68

EX-69

P-36

EX-70

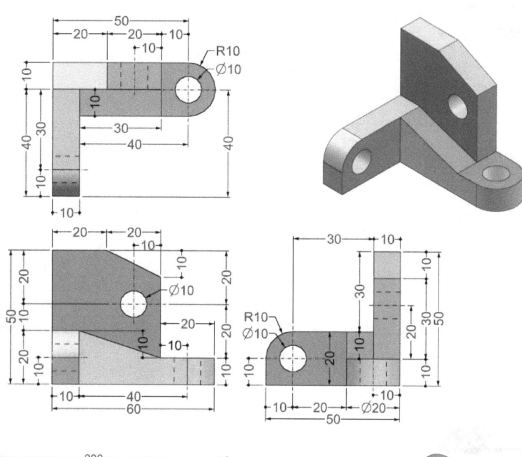

EX-71

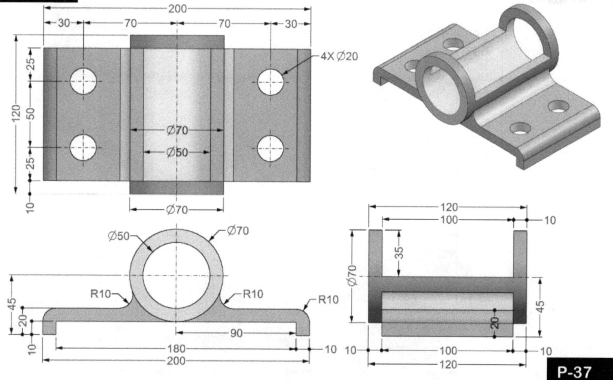

P-37

EX-72

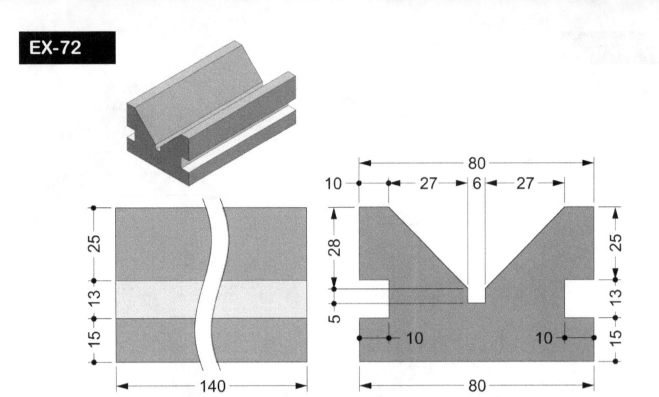

EX-73

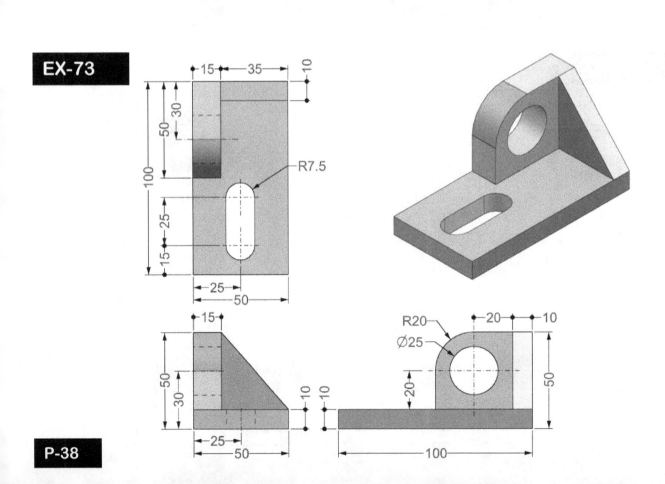

P-38

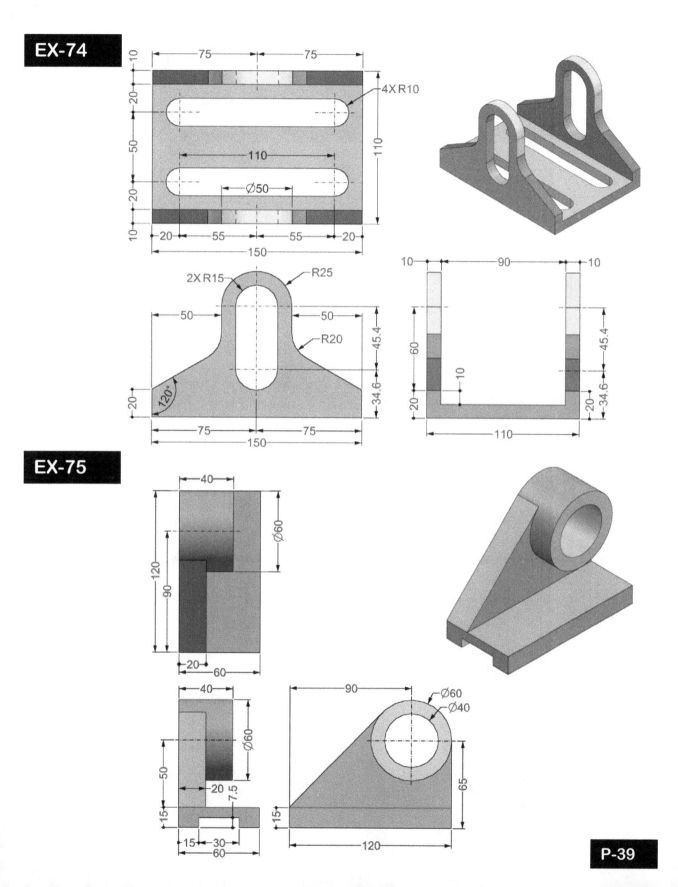

EX-74

4X R10

110

10
75
75
20
50
20
10
20
55
55
20
150
Ø50
110

2X R15
R25
50
50
R20
45.4
34.6
120°
20
75
75
150

10
90
10
60
10
45.4
20
20
34.6
110

EX-75

40
Ø60
120
90
20
60

40
Ø60
50
20
7.5
15
15
30
60

90
Ø60
Ø40
65
15
120

P-39

EX-76

EX-77

SECTION A-A

P-40

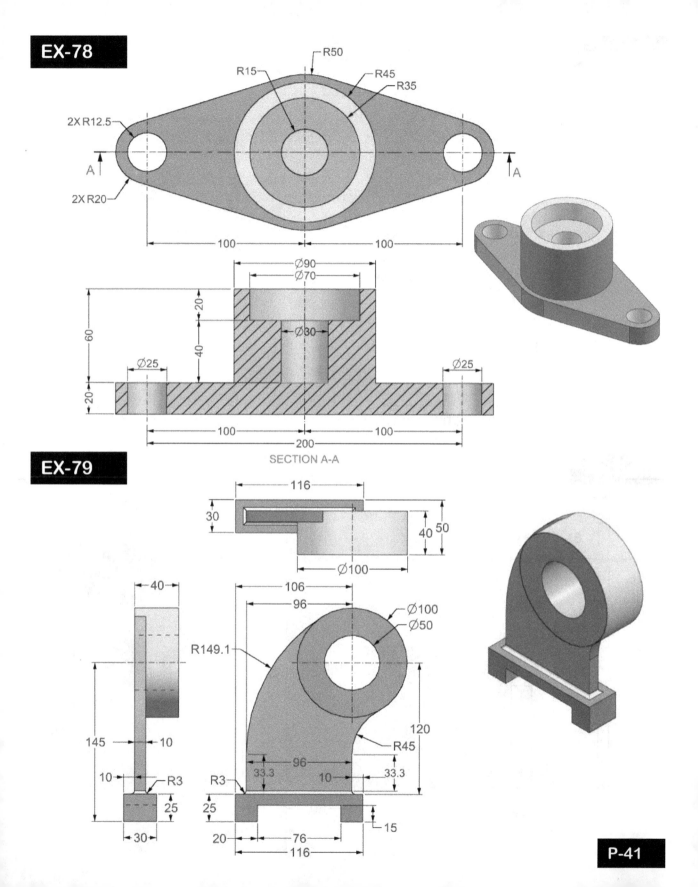

EX-78

R50
R15
R45
R35
2X R12.5
2X R20
A
A
100
100

∅90
∅70
20
60
40
∅30
∅25
∅25
20
100
100
200

SECTION A-A

EX-79

116
30
40
50
∅100

106
96
∅100
∅50
R149.1
40
120
R45
145
10
96
33.3
10
33.3
10
R3
R3
25
25
30
15
20
76
116

P-41

4 HOLES, Ø8.6
ON DIA 54 PCD

6 HOLES, Ø10
ON DIA 32 PCD

Ø70

Ø16

A

A

Ø54

Ø32

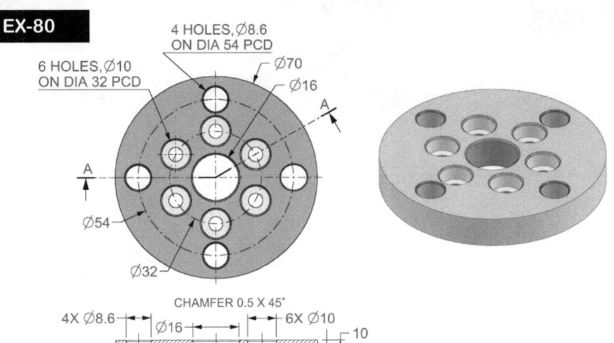

CHAMFER 0.5 X 45°

4X Ø8.6   Ø16   6X Ø10   10

5   5

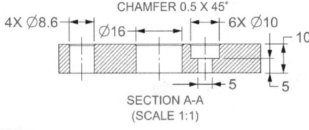

SECTION A-A
(SCALE 1:1)

207.2

171.6   17.8

10

6X Ø8.4

87.2

4X R19.4

19.2

106

9.6

254

254

233.6

190.4

109.8

56.4   36.6

38   28

10

2X R11.6

60   10

103.6

147.2

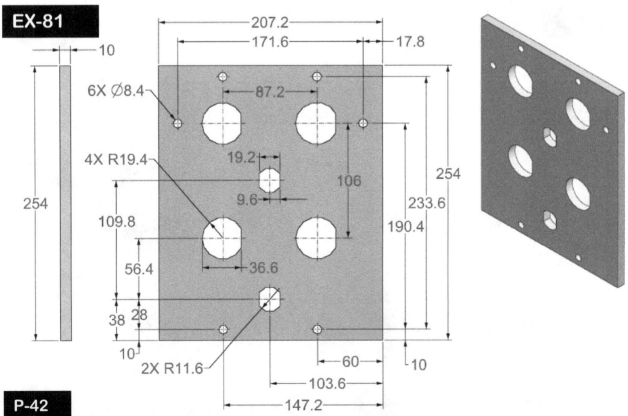

EX-82

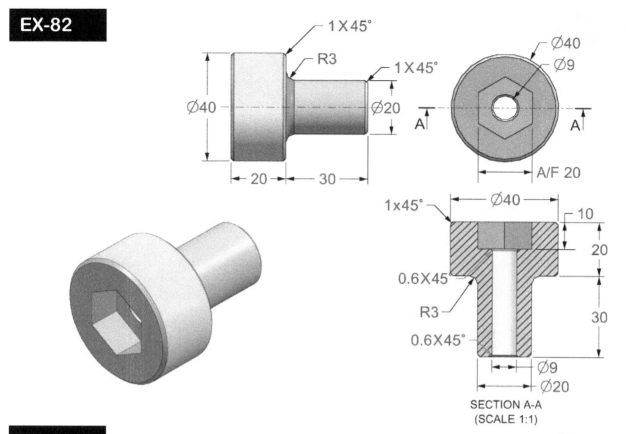

1 X 45°
R3
1 X 45°
Ø40
Ø20
20
30
Ø40
Ø9
A
A
A/F 20

1x45°
Ø40
10
20
0.6X45
R3
30
0.6X45°
Ø9
Ø20

SECTION A-A
(SCALE 1:1)

EX-83

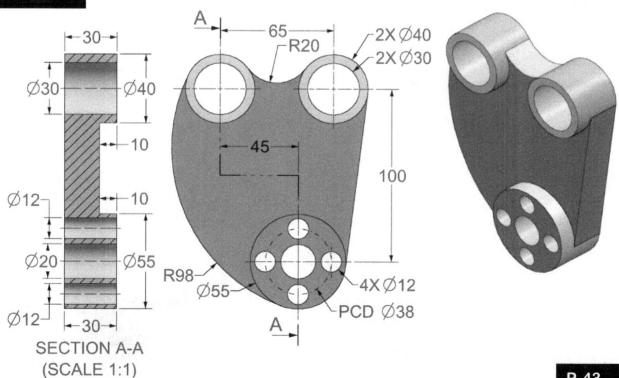

30
Ø30
Ø40
10
10
Ø12
Ø20
Ø55
Ø12
R98
30

SECTION A-A
(SCALE 1:1)

A
65
R20
2X Ø40
2X Ø30
45
100
Ø55
4X Ø12
PCD Ø38
A

EX-84

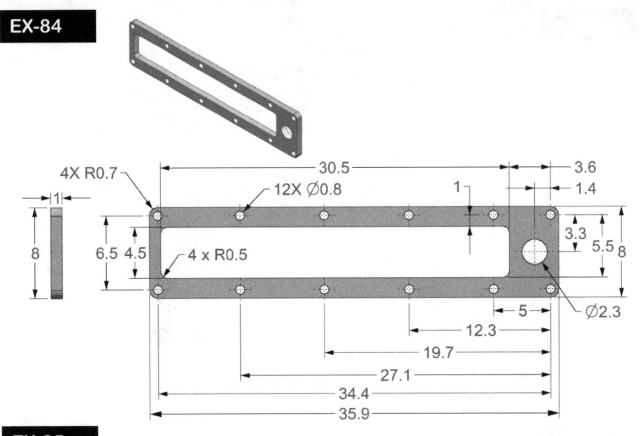

4X R0.7

12X ∅0.8

1

3.6

1.4

1

8

4.5

6.5

4 x R0.5

3.3

5.5

8

30.5

∅2.3

5

12.3

19.7

27.1

34.4

35.9

EX-85

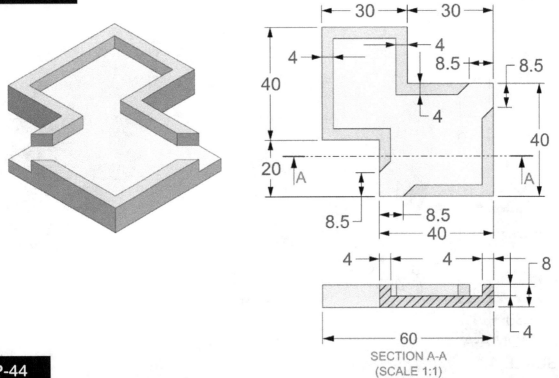

30

30

4

4

8.5

8.5

40

4

40

20

A

A

8.5

8.5

40

4

4

8

60

8.5

SECTION A-A
(SCALE 1:1)

P-44

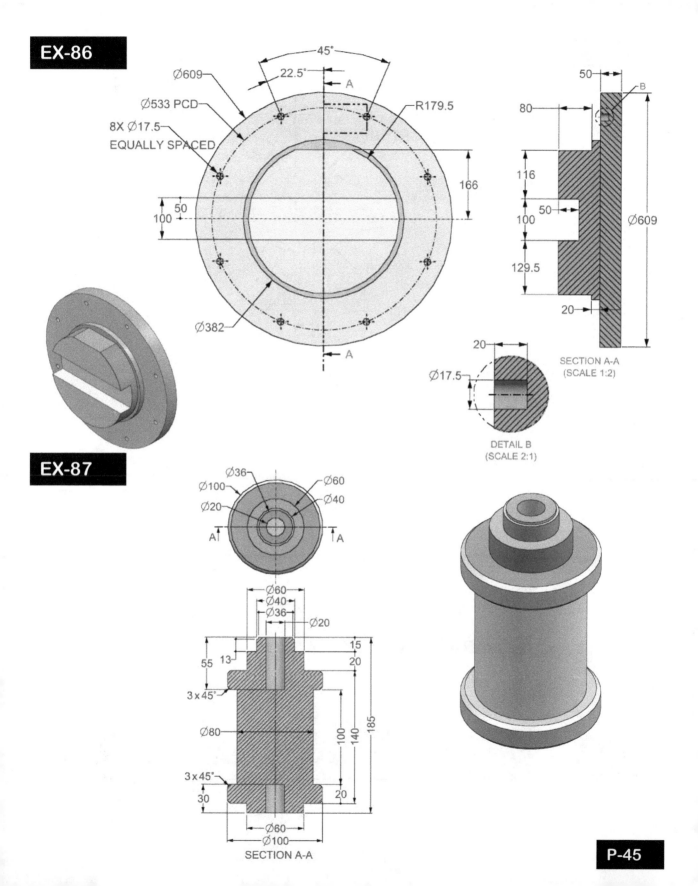

EX-86

Ø609
Ø533 PCD
8X Ø17.5
EQUALLY SPACED
45°
22.5°
A
R179.5
166
50
100
Ø382

50
80
B
116
50
100
129.5
20
Ø609

SECTION A-A
(SCALE 1:2)

20
Ø17.5
DETAIL B
(SCALE 2:1)

EX-87

Ø36
Ø100
Ø60
Ø20
Ø40
A
A

Ø60
Ø40
Ø36
Ø20
15
20
13
55
3 x 45°
Ø80
100
140
185
3 x 45°
30
20
Ø60
Ø100
SECTION A-A

P-45

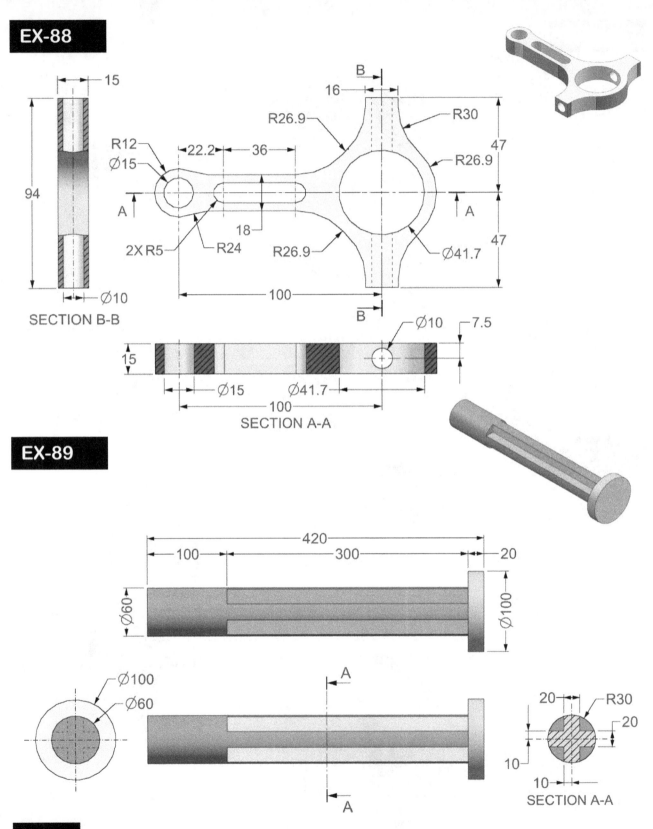

EX-88

15

R12
Ø15
R26.9
R30
47
R26.9
22.2
36
94
16
B
A
A
18
2X R5
R24
R26.9
Ø41.7
47
Ø10
100
B
SECTION B-B

Ø10
7.5
15
Ø15
Ø41.7
100
SECTION A-A

EX-89

420
100
300
20
Ø60
Ø100

Ø100
Ø60
A
A
20
R30
20
10
10
SECTION A-A

P-46

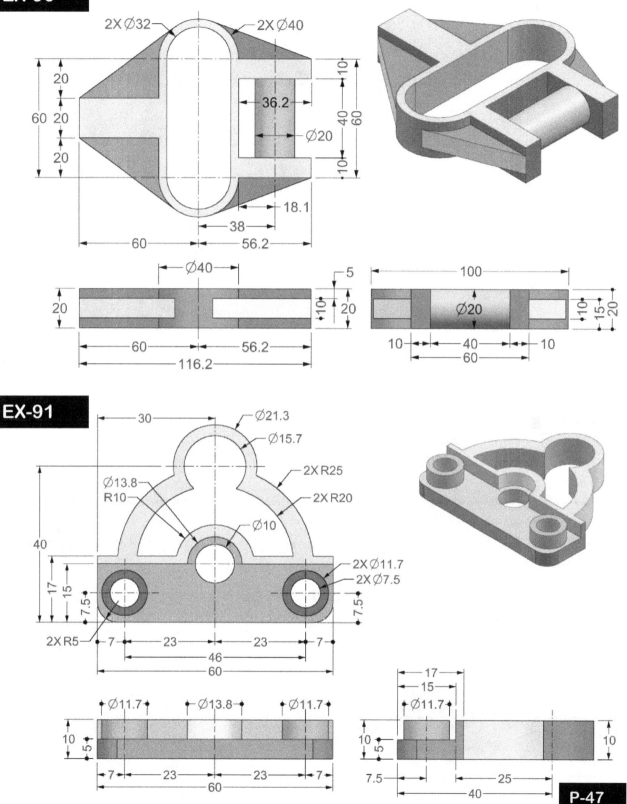

EX-90

2X Ø32 2X Ø40
20
60 20
20
36.2
Ø20
10
40
60
10
18.1
38
60 56.2

Ø40
20
10
20
60 56.2
116.2

5
100
Ø20
10
15
20
10 40 10
60

EX-91

30
Ø21.3
Ø15.7
2X R25
Ø13.8
R10
2X R20
Ø10
40
17
15
7.5
2X Ø11.7
2X Ø7.5
7.5
2X R5 7 23 23 7
46
60

Ø11.7 Ø13.8 Ø11.7
10
5
7 23 23 7
60

17
15
Ø11.7
10
5
7.5 25
40
10

P-47

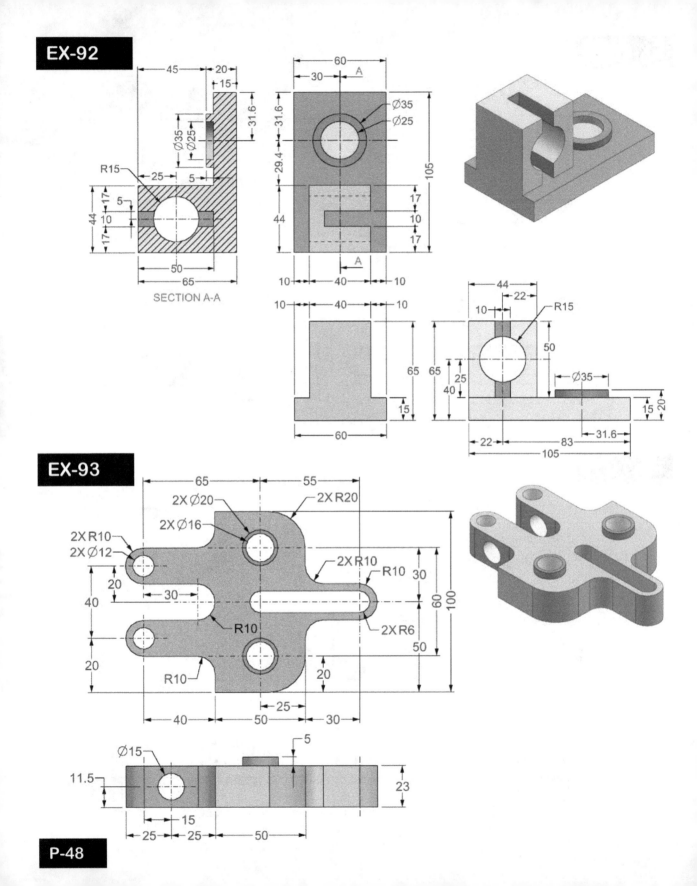

EX-92

SECTION A-A

EX-93

P-48

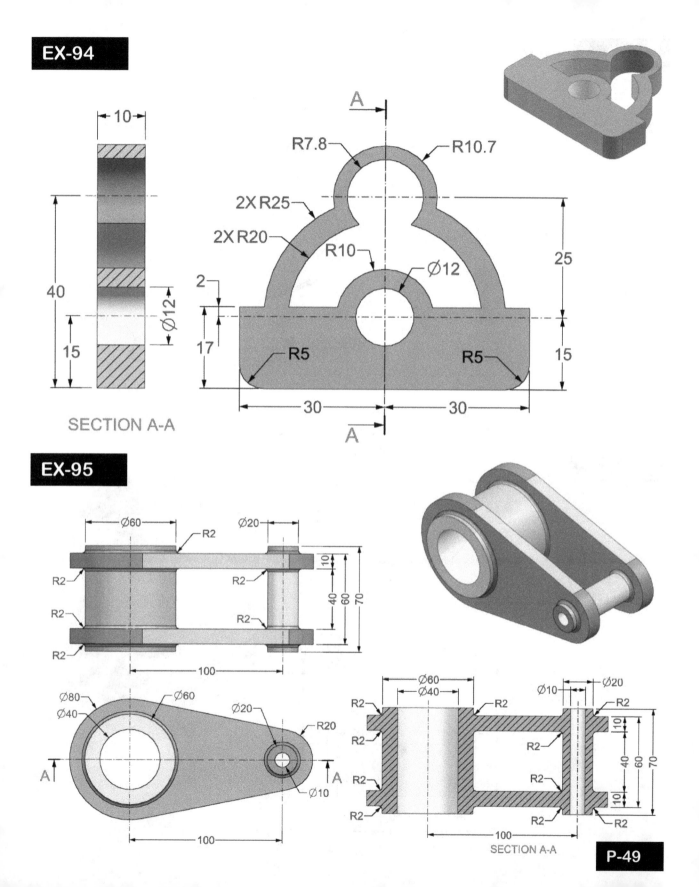

EX-94

R7.8   R10.7

2X R25

2X R20   R10   Ø12

10

40   Ø12

15

SECTION A-A

2

17

R5   R5

30   30

25

15

A
A

EX-95

Ø60   R2   Ø20

R2   R2

R2   R2

R2

10
40
60
70

100

Ø80   Ø60   Ø20   R20
Ø40

A   A

Ø10

100

Ø60   R2   Ø10   Ø20
Ø40

R2   R2   R2

R2

10
40
60
70

R2   R2

R2   R2

100

SECTION A-A

P-49

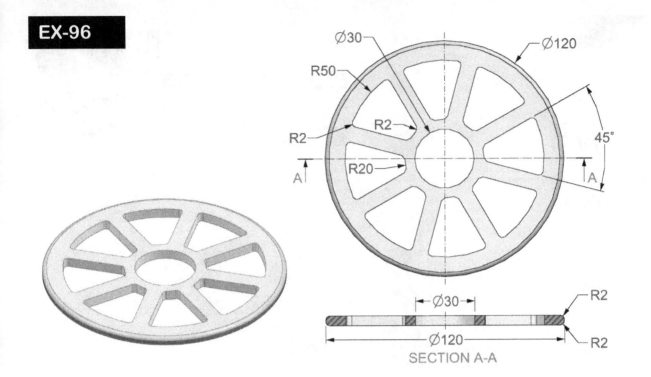

Ø30
R50
R2
R2
R20
Ø120
45°

Ø30
Ø120
R2
R2

SECTION A-A

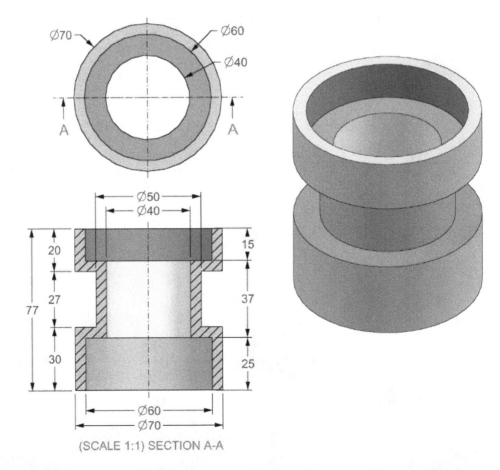

Ø70
Ø60
Ø40

A   A

Ø50
Ø40
20
27
77
30
15
37
25

Ø60
Ø70

(SCALE 1:1) SECTION A-A

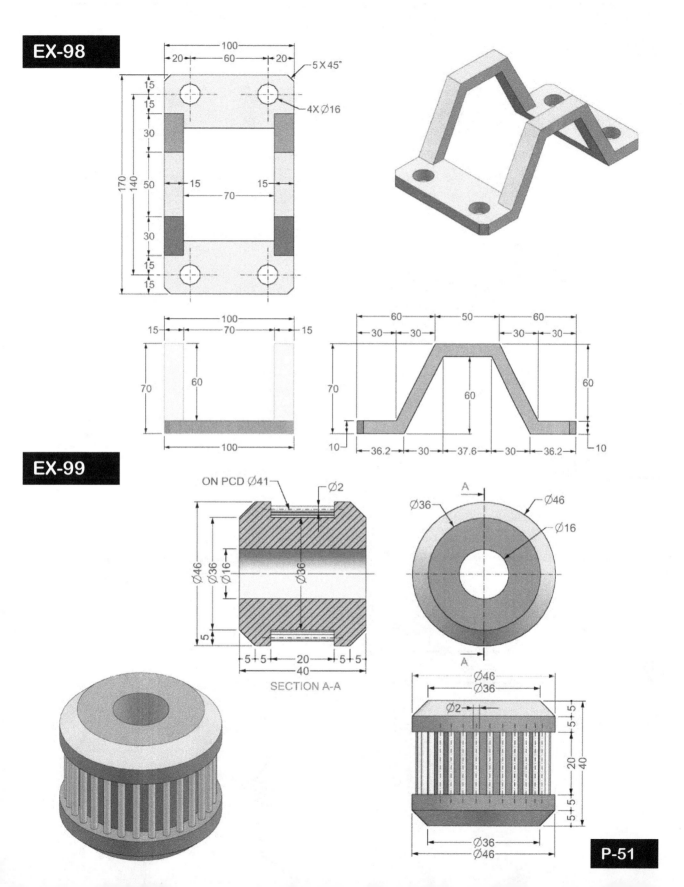

EX-98

100
20 60 20
5 X 45°
15
15
4X⌀16
30
170 140
50 15 15
70
30
15
15

100
15 70 15
70 60
100

60 50 60
30 30 30 30
70 60
60
10 10
36.2 30 37.6 30 36.2

EX-99

ON PCD ⌀41
⌀2
⌀46 ⌀36 ⌀16
⌀36
5
5 5 20 5 5
40
SECTION A-A

A
⌀36
⌀46
⌀16
A

⌀46
⌀36
⌀2
5 5
5 5
20 40
5 5
⌀36
⌀46

P-51

EX-100

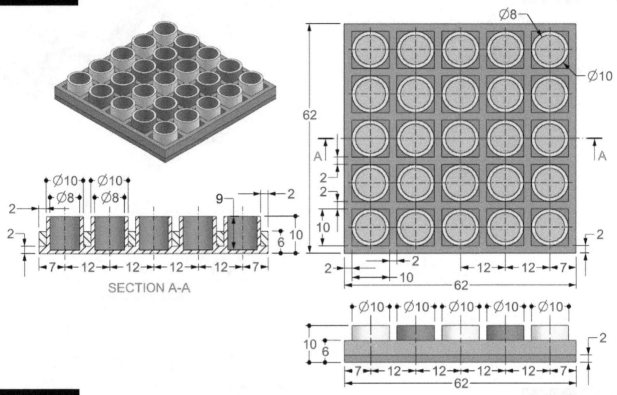

SECTION A-A

EX-101

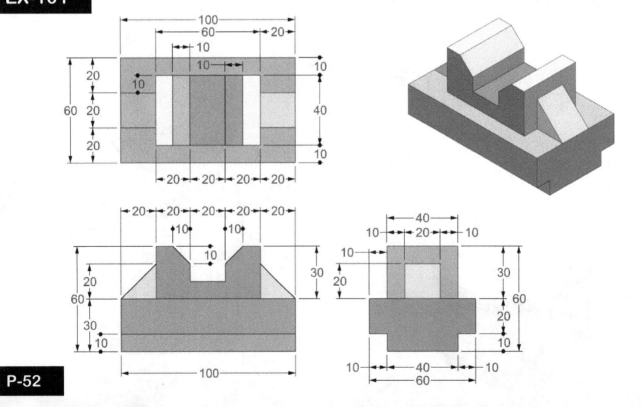

P-52

EX-102

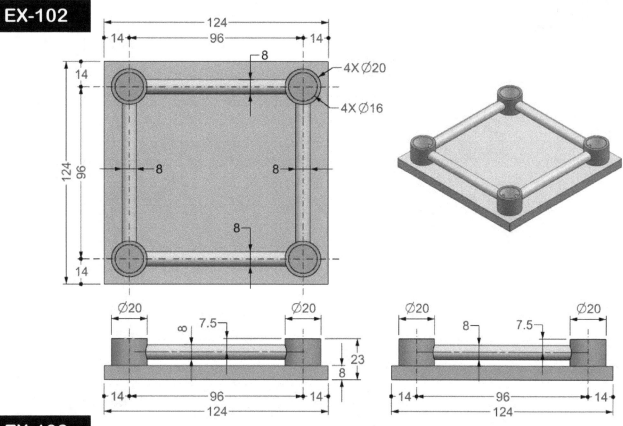

EX-103

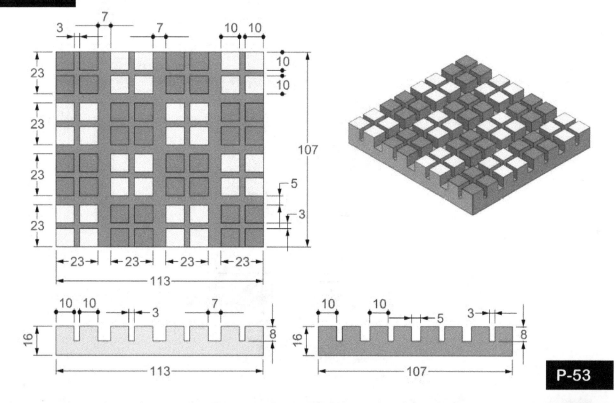

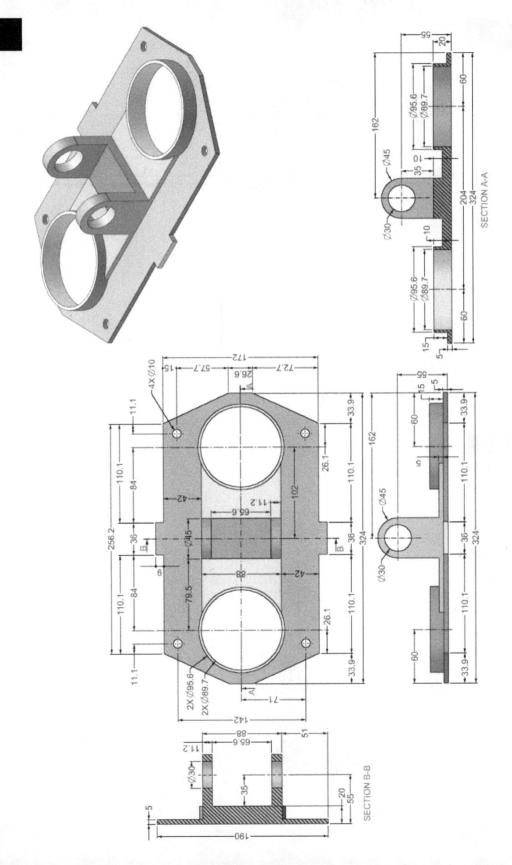

SECTION A-A

SECTION B-B

EX-105

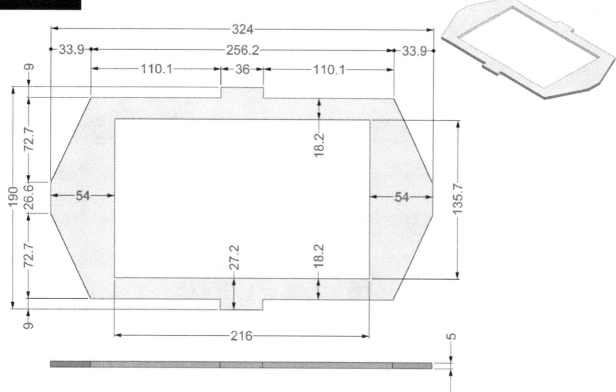

EX-106

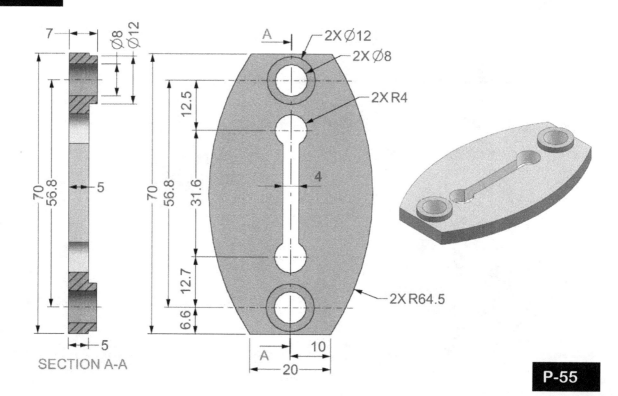

SECTION A-A

EX-107

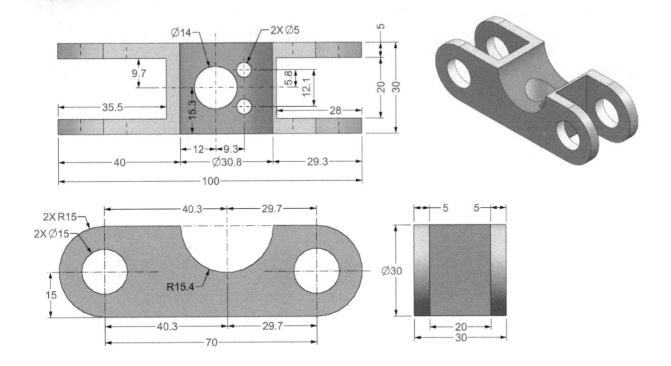

EX-108

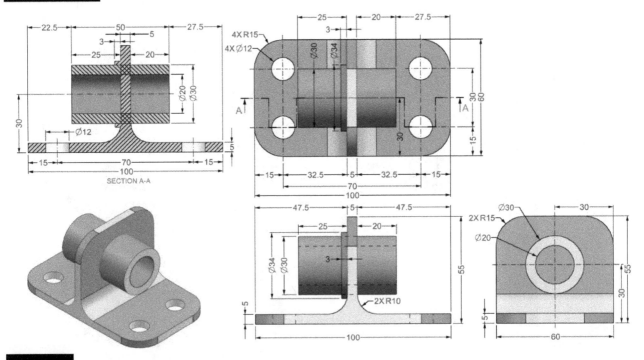

SECTION A-A

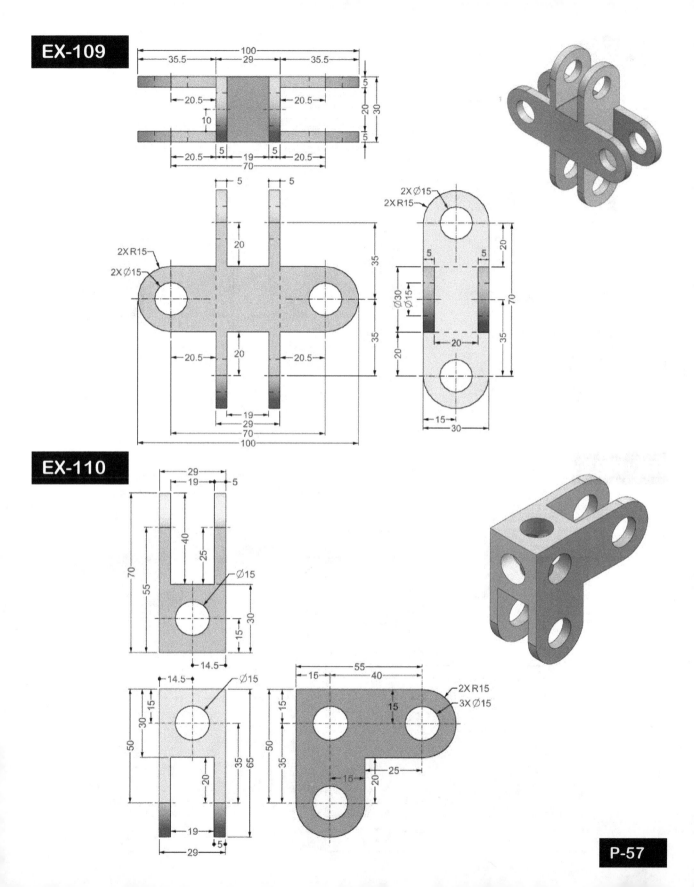

EX-109

EX-110

P-57

EX-111

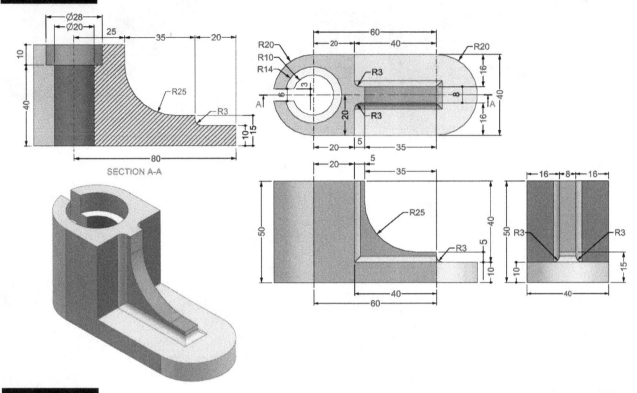

SECTION A-A

EX-112

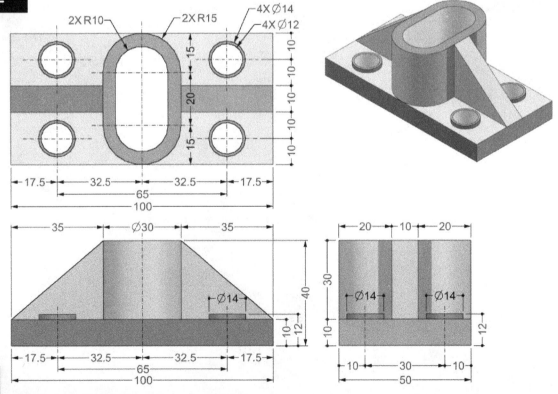

EX-113

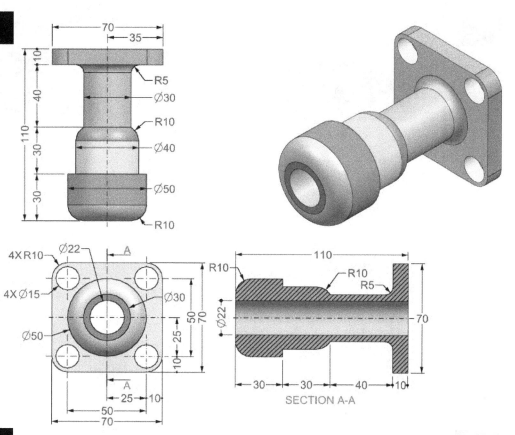

4X R10 Ø22
4X Ø15
Ø50
Ø30
A
50
70
25
10
A
25 10
50
70

R10
Ø22
R10
R5
110
70
30 30 40 10
SECTION A-A

EX-114

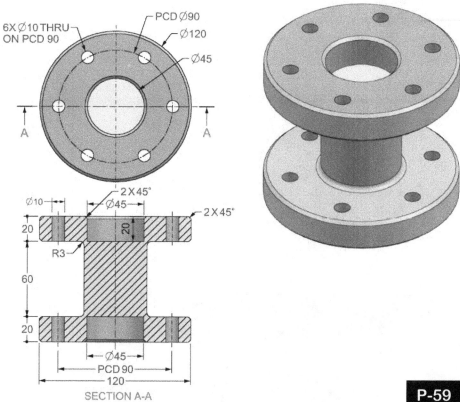

6X Ø10 THRU
ON PCD 90
PCD Ø90
Ø120
Ø45
A
A

Ø10
20
R3
60
20
2 X 45°
Ø45
20
2 X 45°
Ø45
PCD 90
120
SECTION A-A

Ø120
6X Ø10
6X Ø8
PCD Ø90
Ø68
Ø45

A | A

Ø120
Ø68
Ø10
R2
10
10
20
120
60
20
10
PCD 90

Ø120
PCD 90
Ø68
Ø45
Ø10
2 X 45°
20
40
20
R3
60
60
R3
Ø8
Ø55
Ø50
20
20
Ø45
Ø8

SECTION A-A

120
100
10
25
50
25
10
4X Ø10
4X R5
25
A
A
25
30
50
15
10
Ø30
Ø20

20
80
50
45
20
R5
120

80
20
70
25
Ø10
30
R5
20
10
100
120

SECTION A-A

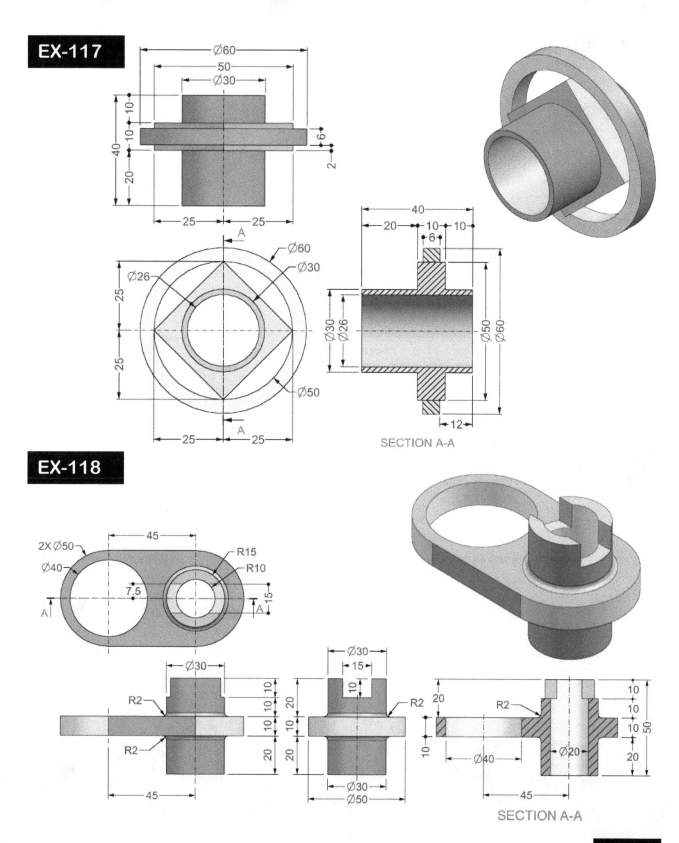

EX-117

Ø60
50
Ø30
10
10
40
20
6
2
25
25

A
Ø60
Ø30
Ø26
25
25
25
25
Ø50
A

40
20
10
10
6
Ø30
Ø26
Ø50
Ø60
12

SECTION A-A

EX-118

2X Ø50
Ø40
45
R15
R10
7.5
15
A
A

R2
Ø30
10
10
10
10
20
20
R2
45

Ø30
15
10
20
10
20
R2
Ø30
Ø50

20
R2
10
Ø40
Ø20
45
10
10
10
20
50

SECTION A-A

P-61

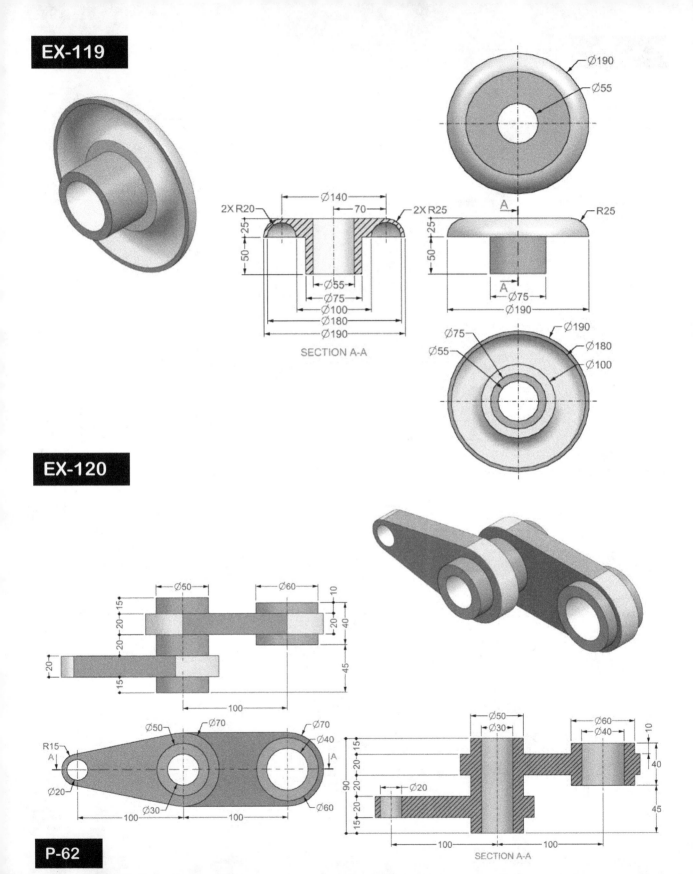

EX-119

Ø190
Ø55

Ø140
70
2X R20
2X R25
25
50
Ø55
Ø75
Ø100
Ø180
Ø190

SECTION A-A

A
25
50
R25
Ø75
Ø190

Ø75
Ø190
Ø55
Ø180
Ø100

EX-120

Ø50
Ø60
10
15
20
20
20
40
20
20
45
15
100

Ø50
Ø70
Ø70
R15
A
Ø40
Ø20
Ø30
Ø60
100
100

Ø50
Ø30
Ø60
Ø40
10
15
20
20
40
90
20
20
Ø20
20
15
45
100
100

SECTION A-A

P-62

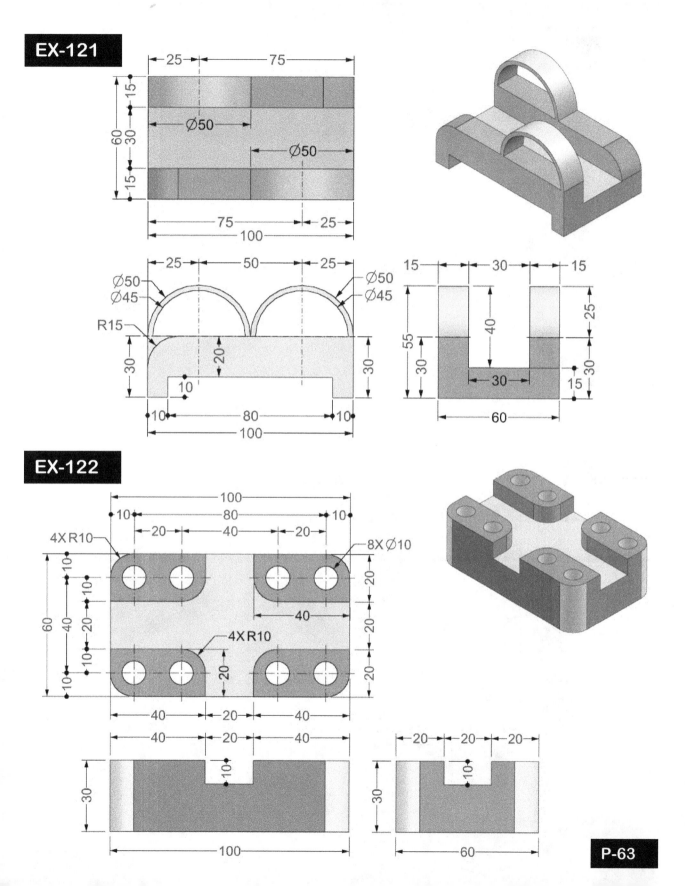

EX-121

EX-122

P-63

EX-123

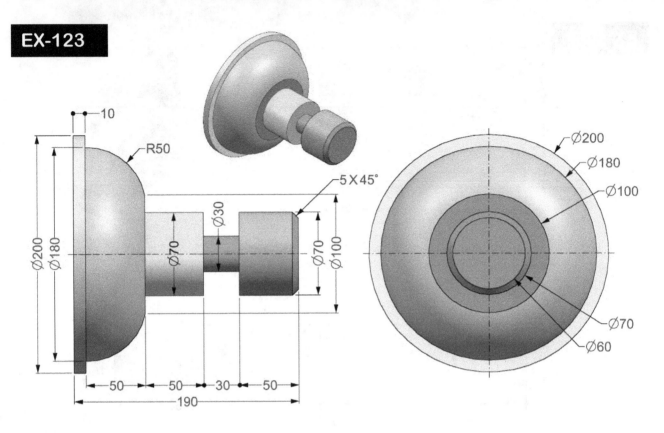

- 10
- R50
- 5 × 45°
- Ø30
- Ø70
- Ø70
- Ø100
- Ø200
- Ø180
- 50
- 50
- 30
- 50
- 190
- Ø200
- Ø180
- Ø100
- Ø70
- Ø60

EX-124

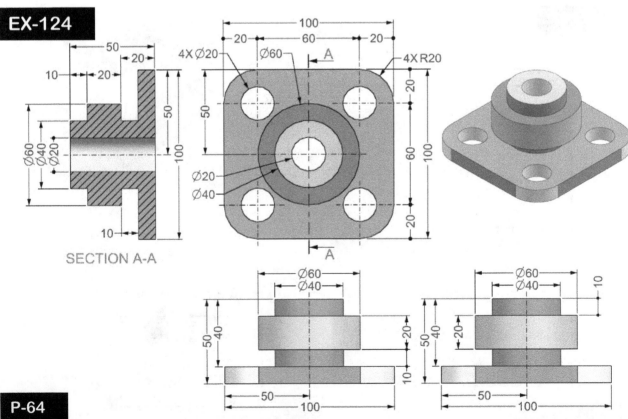

- 50
- 20
- 10
- 20
- Ø60
- Ø40
- Ø20
- 10
- 100
- 20
- 60
- 20
- 4X Ø20
- Ø60
- A
- 4X R20
- 50
- 20
- 60
- 20
- 100
- Ø20
- Ø40
- A
- SECTION A-A
- Ø60
- Ø40
- 50
- 40
- 20
- 10
- 50
- 100
- Ø60
- Ø40
- 10
- 50
- 40
- 20
- 50
- 100

EX-125

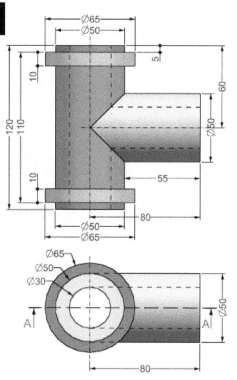

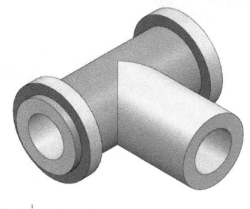

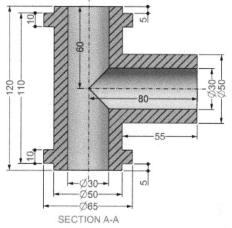

SECTION A-A

EX-126

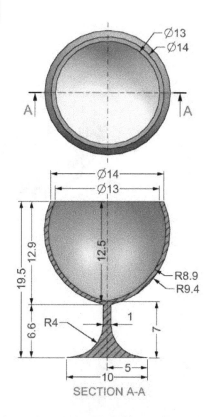

SECTION A-A

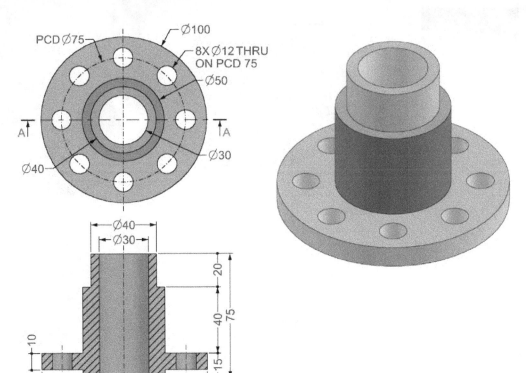

PCD Ø75
Ø100
8X Ø12 THRU
ON PCD 75
Ø50
A
A
Ø40
Ø30

Ø40
Ø30
20
75
40
10
15
Ø50
75
Ø100
SECTION A-A

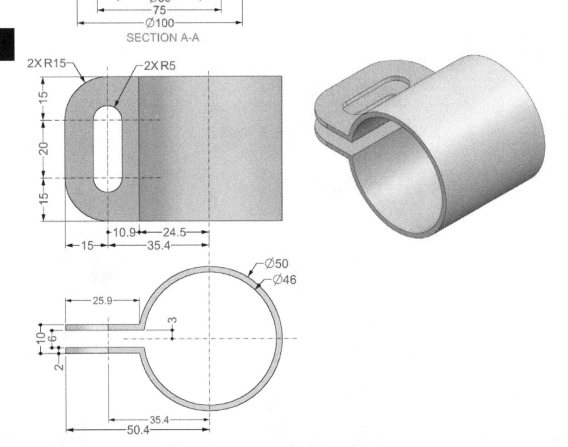

2X R15
2X R5
15
20
15
10.9
24.5
15
35.4

25.9
3
10
6
2
Ø50
Ø46
35.4
50.4

EX-129

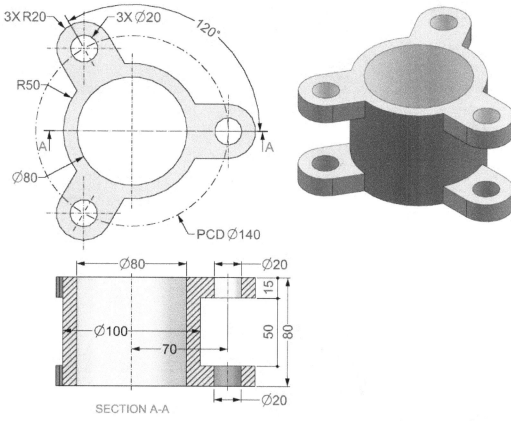

3X R20 3X Ø20 120°

R50

Ø80

A   A

PCD Ø140

Ø80   Ø20

15

Ø100

70   50   80

Ø20

SECTION A-A

EX-130

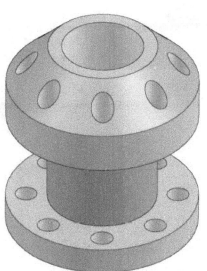

PCD Ø55   Ø70

A   A

8X Ø8
ON PCD 55

Ø30   Ø40

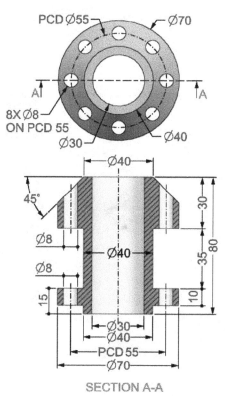

Ø40

45°

30

Ø8

Ø40

80

35

Ø8

15

10

Ø30
Ø40
PCD 55
Ø70

SECTION A-A

P-67

EX-131

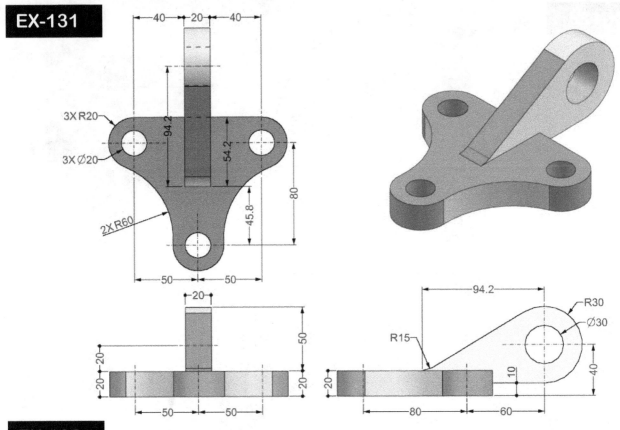

EX-132

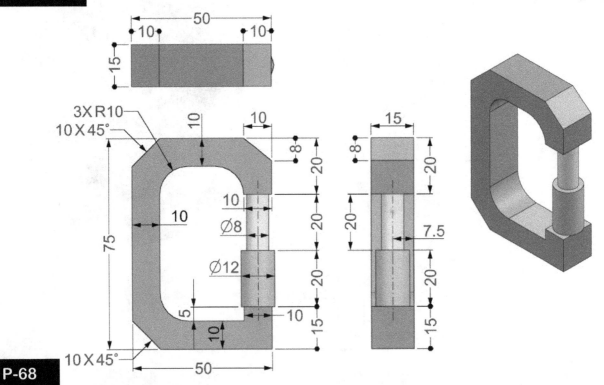

P-68

EX-133

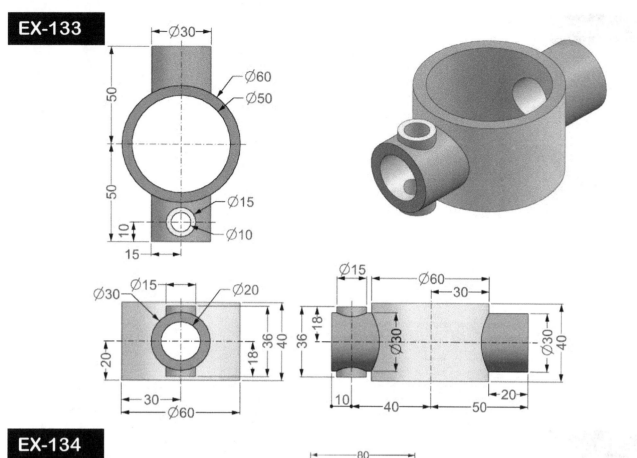

EX-134

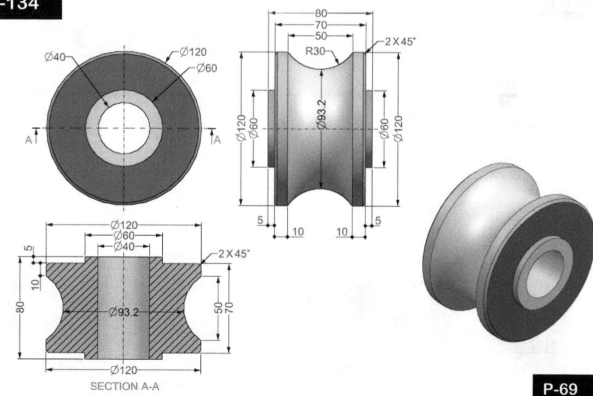

SECTION A-A

P-69

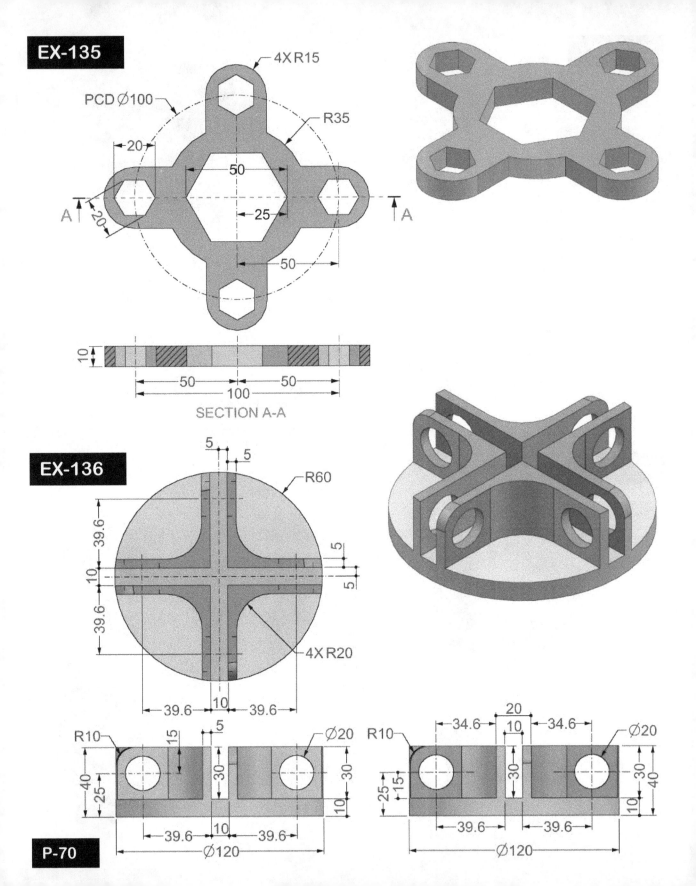

EX-135

4X R15

PCD Ø100

R35

20

50

25

50

50

A

A

10

50 50

100

SECTION A-A

EX-136

5

5

R60

39.6

5

10

5

39.6

4X R20

39.6 10 39.6

R10

15

5

Ø20

40

25

30

30

10

39.6 10 39.6

Ø120

R10

20

34.6 10 34.6

Ø20

25

15

30

30

40

10

39.6 39.6

Ø120

P-70

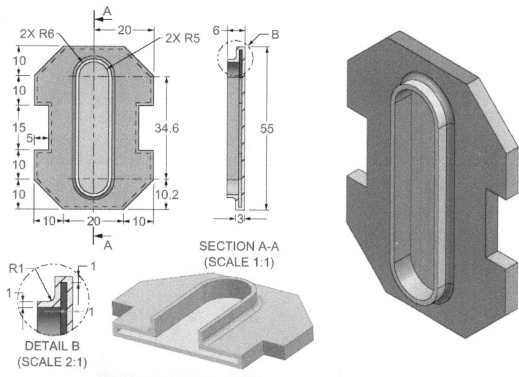

EX-137

2X R6
2X R5
20
6
B
10
10
15
5
34.6
55
10
10
10.2
10 · 20 · 10
3

SECTION A-A
(SCALE 1:1)

R1
1
1
1

DETAIL B
(SCALE 2:1)

SHELL THICKNESS = 1MM
ALL INSIDE WALL THICKNESS

EX-138

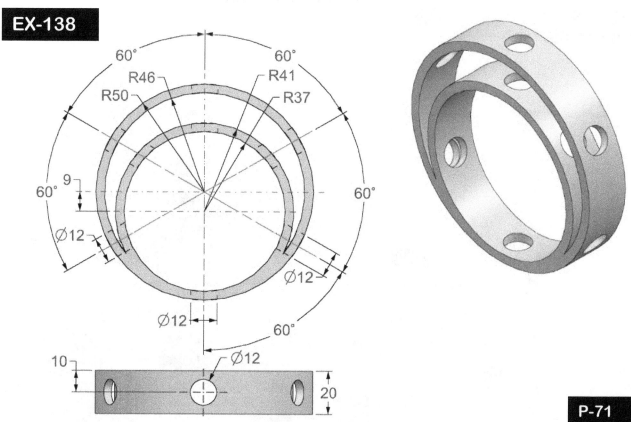

60°
60°
R46
R41
R50
R37
60°
9
60°
Ø12
Ø12
Ø12
60°
Ø12
10
Ø12
20

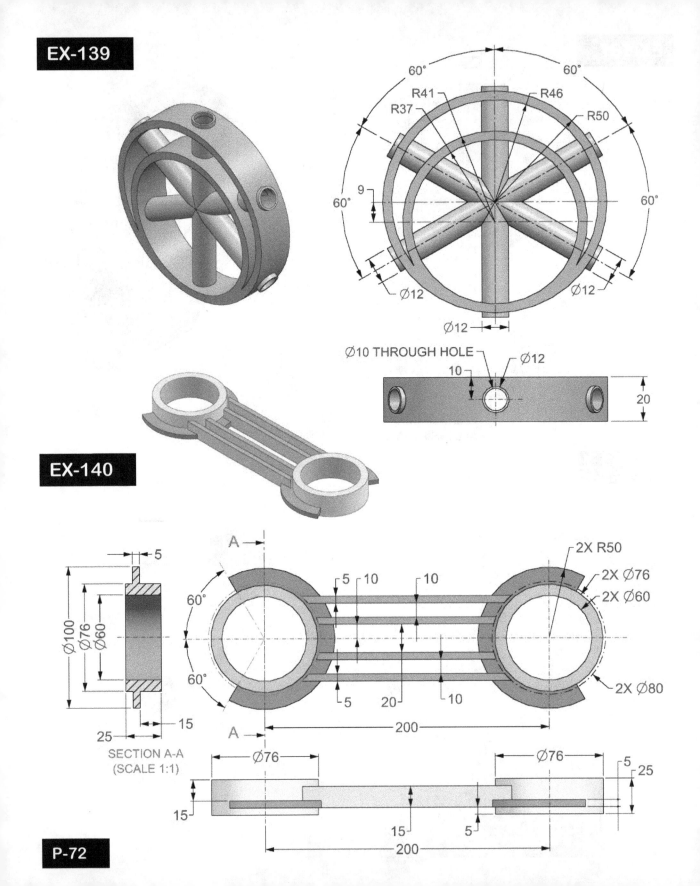

EX-139

R41
R37
R46
R50
60°
60°
60°
60°
9
Ø12
Ø12
Ø12

Ø10 THROUGH HOLE
Ø12
10
20

EX-140

A
2X R50
2X Ø76
2X Ø60
5 10
10
60°
Ø100
Ø76
Ø60
60°
2X Ø80
5
20
10
5
A
200
15
25
SECTION A-A
(SCALE 1:1)
Ø76
Ø76
5
25
15
15
5
200

P-72

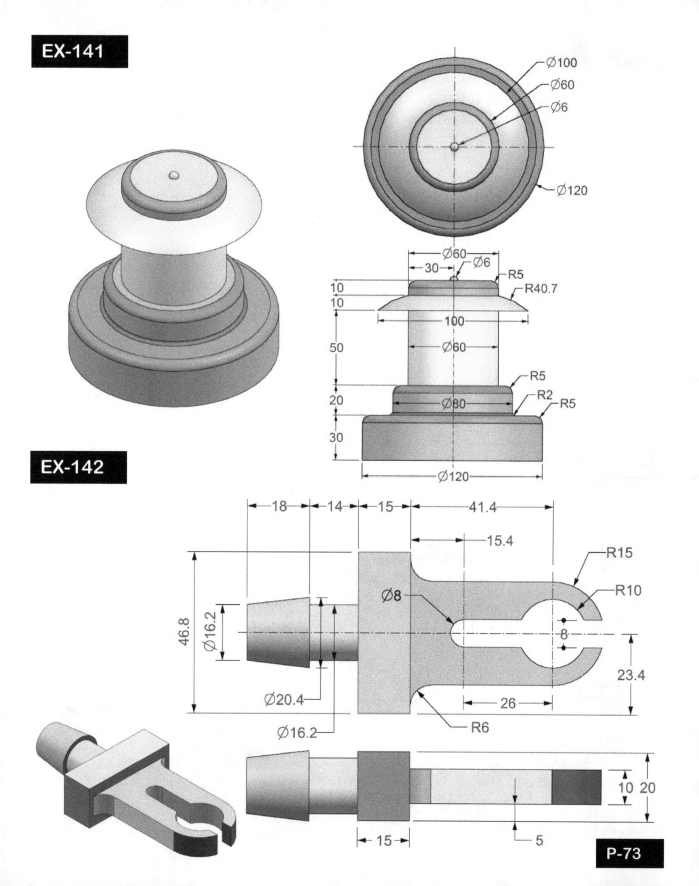

EX-141

Ø100
Ø60
Ø6
Ø120

Ø60
Ø6
30
R5
10
R40.7
10
100
50
Ø60
R5
20
R2 R5
Ø80
30
Ø120

EX-142

18
14
15
41.4
15.4
R15
R10
Ø8
46.8
Ø16.2
8
Ø20.4
23.4
Ø16.2
26
R6

10 20
15
5

P-73

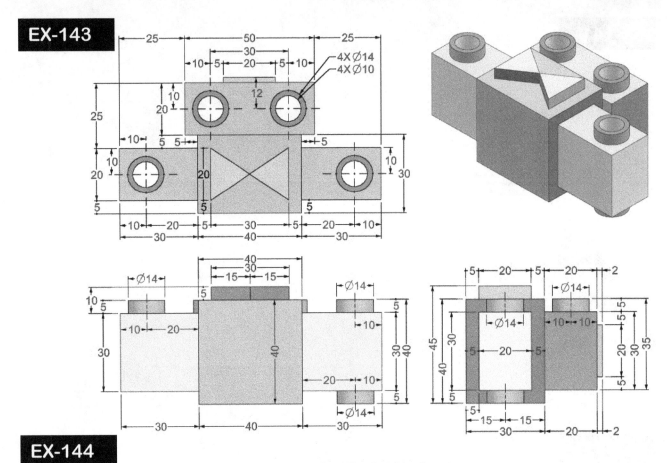

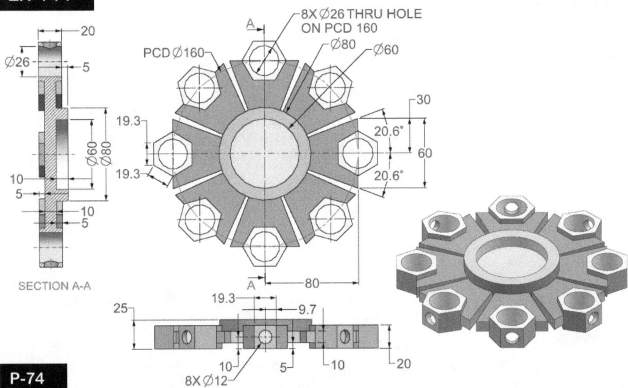

SECTION A-A

8X Ø26 THRU HOLE ON PCD 160

PCD Ø160

Ø80

Ø60

8X Ø12

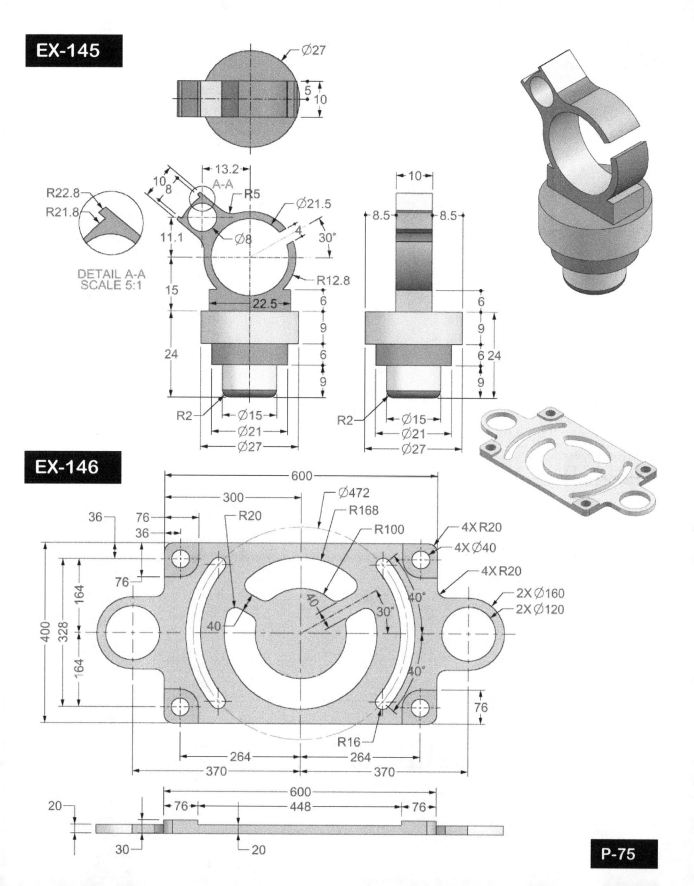

EX-145

Ø27

5
10

13.2
A-A
10
8
R5
Ø21.5
R22.8
R21.8
11.1
Ø8
4
30°
R12.8
15
22.5
DETAIL A-A
SCALE 5:1
24
R2
Ø15
Ø21
Ø27

10
8.5
8.5
6
9
6 24
9
R2
Ø15
Ø21
Ø27

EX-146

600
Ø472
300
R168
R20
R100
4X R20
36
76
4X Ø40
36
4X R20
76
2X Ø160
164
40
2X Ø120
400
328
40°
40
30°
164
40°
76
40
264
264
R16
370
370

600
76
448
76
20
30
20

P-75

Ø40
120°
Ø20
120°
10
60

R10
Ø40
200
79.6
Ø20
15
R15
60

2X Ø100
Ø50
2X Ø80
R45
51.6
R40
Ø30
100
100

Ø90
Ø50
10
10
40
15
100
100

Ø90
Ø80
Ø80
Ø50
Ø30
Ø80
15
10
40
10
100
100
15

SECTION A-A

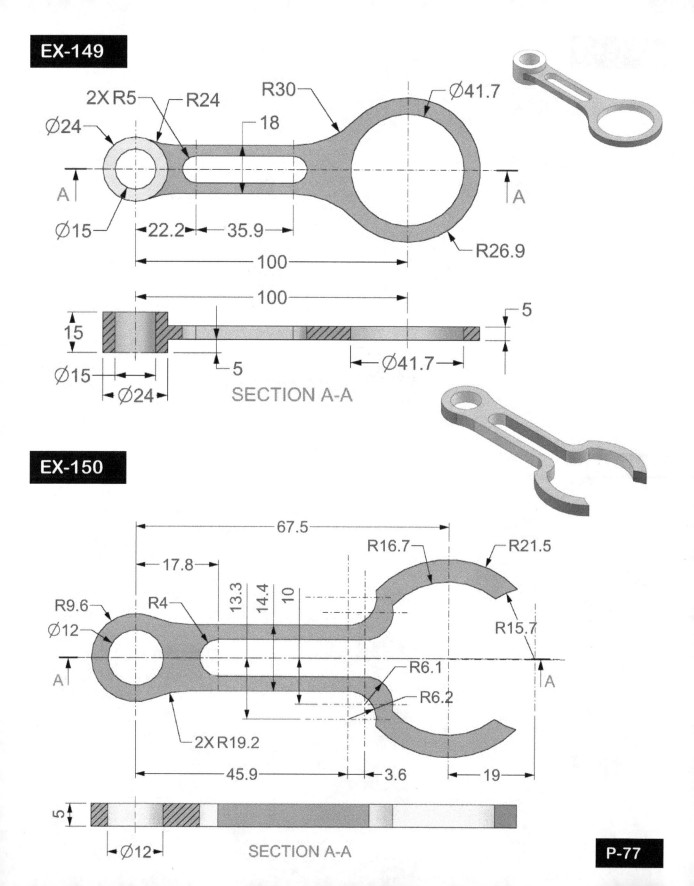

EX-149

2X R5 — R24
Ø24
R30
Ø41.7
18
A
A
Ø15
2X R5
22.2
35.9
100

100
15
Ø15
Ø24
5
5
Ø41.7
SECTION A-A

EX-150

67.5
17.8
R16.7
R21.5
13.3
14.4
10
R9.6
R4
Ø12
A
A
R15.7
R6.1
R6.2
2X R19.2
45.9
3.6
19

5
Ø12
SECTION A-A

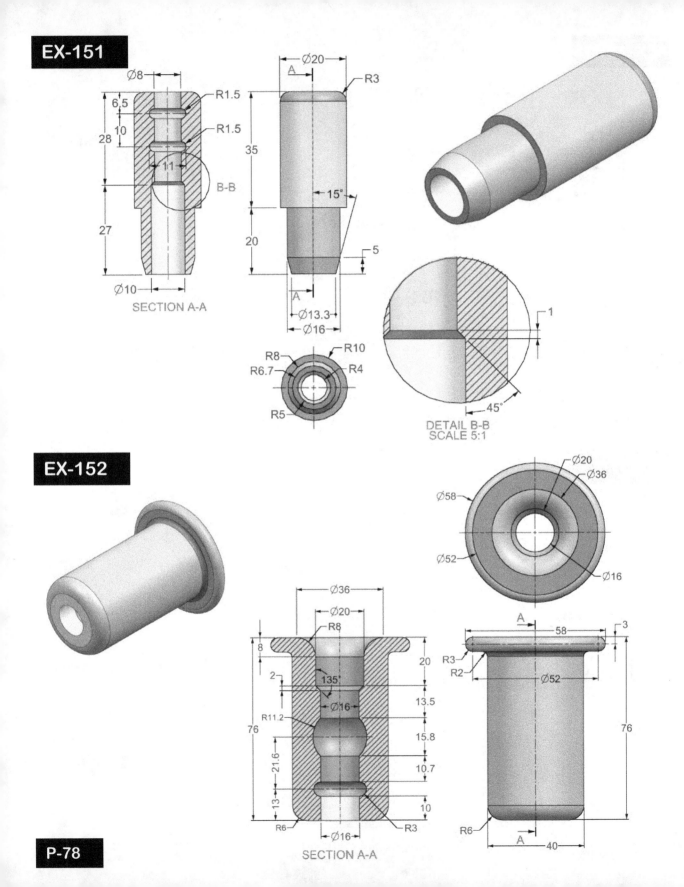

EX-151

Ø8
6.5
10
28
R1.5
R1.5
1:1
B-B
27
Ø10
SECTION A-A

Ø20
A
R3
35
15°
20
5
A
Ø13.3
Ø16

R8
R10
R6.7
R4
R5

1
45°
DETAIL B-B
SCALE 5:1

EX-152

Ø20
Ø36
Ø58
Ø52
Ø16

Ø36
Ø20
R8
8
135°
2
Ø16
20
R11.2
13.5
76
15.8
21.6
10.7
13
10
R6
Ø16
R3
SECTION A-A

A
58
3
R3
R2
Ø52
76
R6
A
40

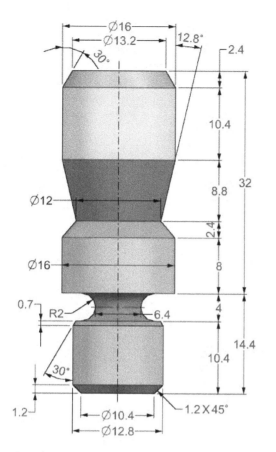

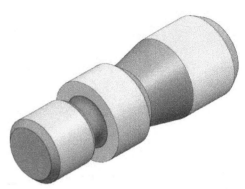

Ø16
Ø13.2
12.8°
30°
2.4
10.4
8.8
2.4
32
Ø12
8
Ø16
0.7
R2
6.4
4
14.4
10.4
30°
1.2 X 45°
1.2
Ø10.4
Ø12.8

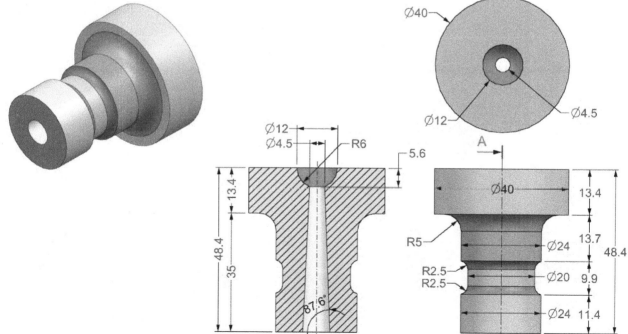

Ø40
Ø12
Ø4.5
Ø12
Ø4.5
R6
5.6
A
13.4
Ø40
13.4
48.4
R5
13.7
Ø24
35
R2.5
R2.5
Ø20
9.9
48.4
87.6°
Ø24
11.4
Ø8
A

SECTION A-A

EX-155

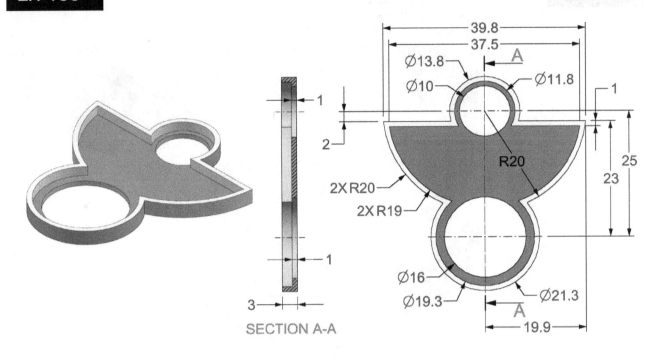

SECTION A-A

EX-156

SECTION A-A

P-80

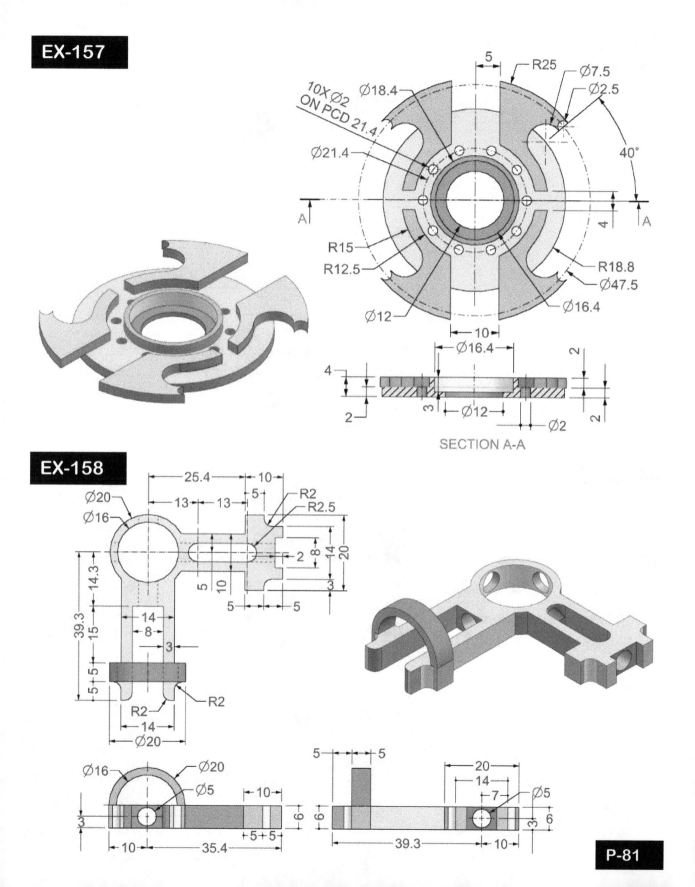

EX-157

10X Ø2
ON PCD 21.4

Ø18.4
Ø21.4
5
R25
Ø7.5
Ø2.5
40°
4
R15
R12.5
Ø12
R18.8
Ø47.5
Ø16.4
10
Ø16.4
4
2
2
3
Ø12
Ø2
2

SECTION A-A

EX-158

25.4
10
13
13
5
R2
R2.5
Ø20
Ø16
2
8
14
20
5
10
3
5
5
14
14.3
8
39.3
3
15
5 5
R2
R2
14
Ø20

Ø16
Ø20
Ø5
10
3
10
35.4
5 5
6

5
5
20
14
7
Ø5
6
6
3
39.3
10

P-81

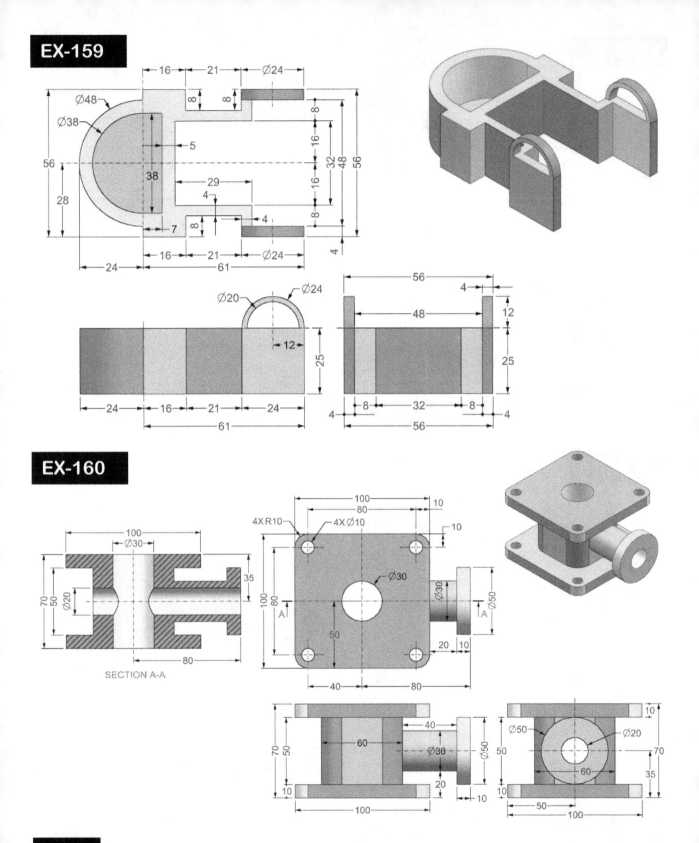

EX-159

EX-160

SECTION A-A

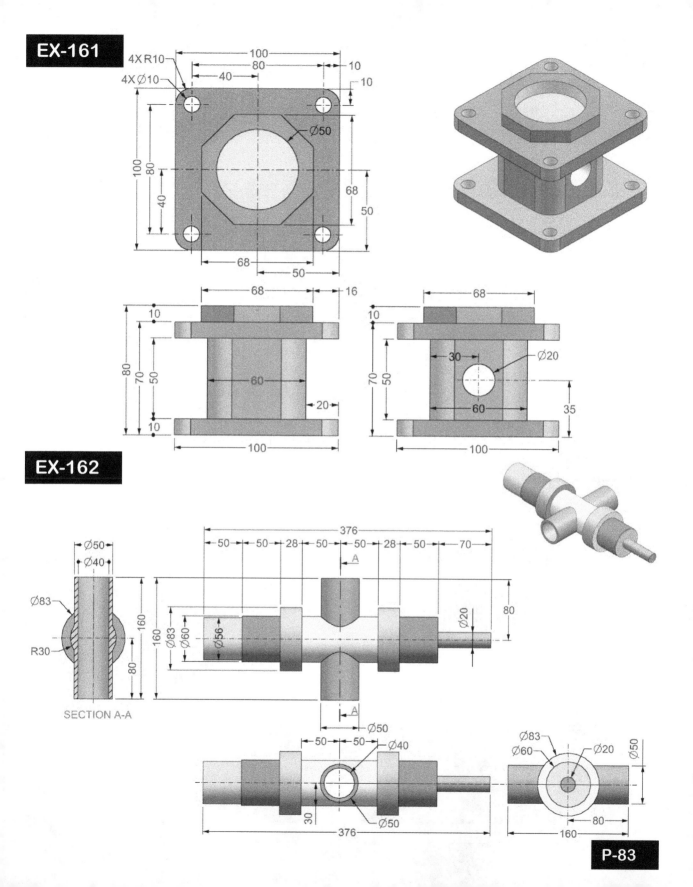

EX-161

EX-162

SECTION A-A

P-83

EX-163

10

Ø20

Ø20

Ø20

Ø20

10

20

SECTION A-A

PCD Ø160
4X Ø20
2X Ø20
2X R10
Ø20
PCD Ø80.5
Ø120

A
R100
Ø40
B
2X Ø14 THRU HOLES
A

TOP VIEW

10

20

Ø10

SECTION B-B

C

Ø20
Ø40

10
Ø20
Ø20
Ø20
20

C

BOTTOM VIEW

SECTION C-C

EX-164

68
28.2
4X R10
4X Ø10
10
Ø50
Ø30
68
28.2
A
A
80
100
40
10
10
40
40
10
80
100

16
68
16
28.2
10 10
80
70
50
Ø18
25
30
10
60
50
35
100

100
68
Ø50
10 10
10
50
Ø18
25
Ø30
10
50
50
100

SECTION A-A

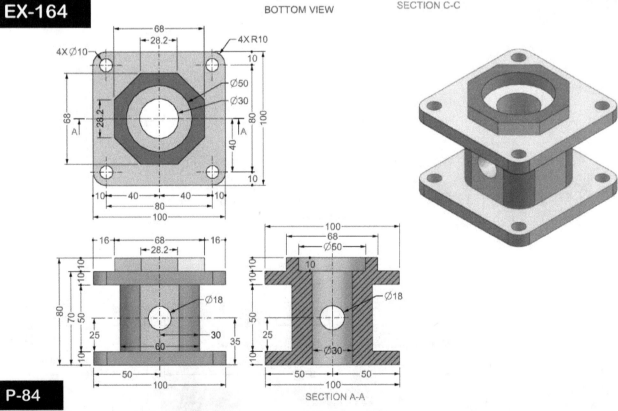

P-84

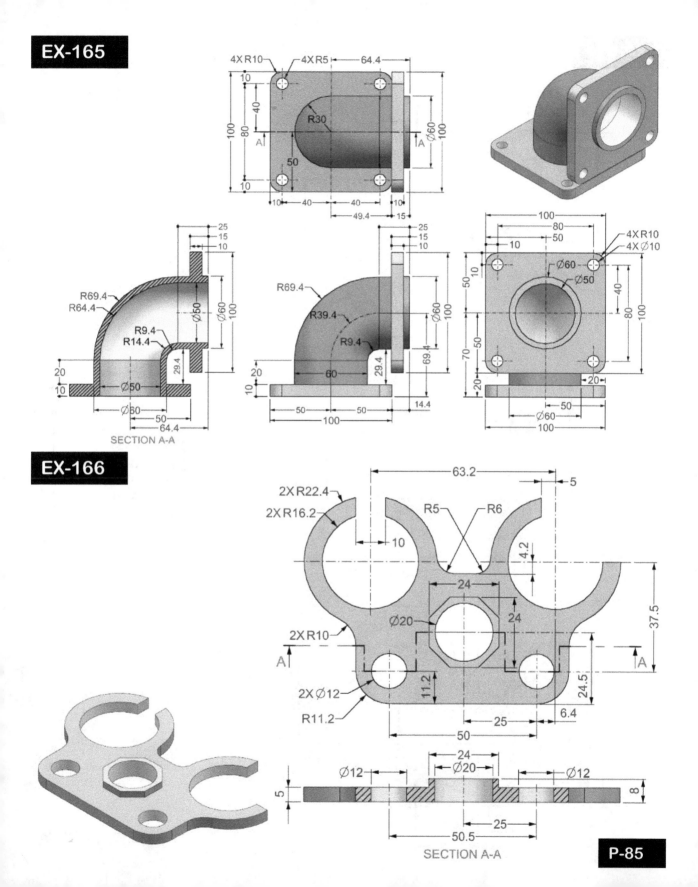

EX-165

4X R10   4X R5   64.4

10
40
100
80
R30
Ø60
100
50
A   A
10
10   40   40   10
49.4   15

25
15
10
R69.4
R64.4
Ø50
Ø60
100
R9.4
R14.4
29.4
20
10
Ø50
Ø60
50
64.4
SECTION A-A

25
15
10
R69.4
R39.4
Ø60
100
R9.4
29.4
69.4
20
10
60
14.4
50   50
100

100
80
50
10
4X R10
4X Ø10
Ø60
Ø50
10
50
40
80
100
70
50
20
20
50
Ø60
100

EX-166

63.2
5
2X R22.4
2X R16.2
R5   R6
10
4.2
24
37.5
Ø20
24
2X R10
A   A
24.5
2X Ø12
11.2
6.4
R11.2
25
50

24
Ø12   Ø20   Ø12
5
8
25
50.5
SECTION A-A

P-85

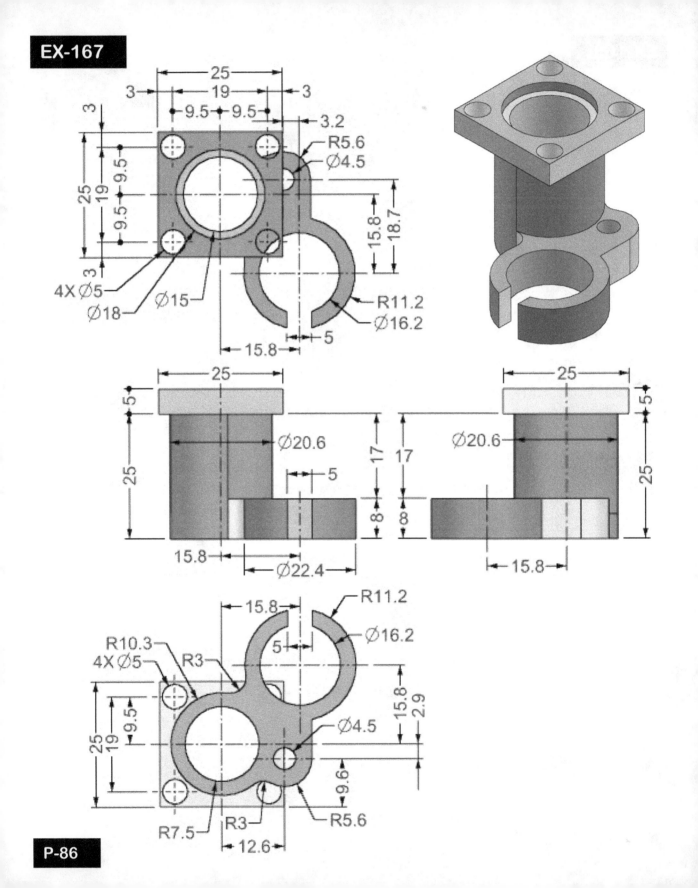

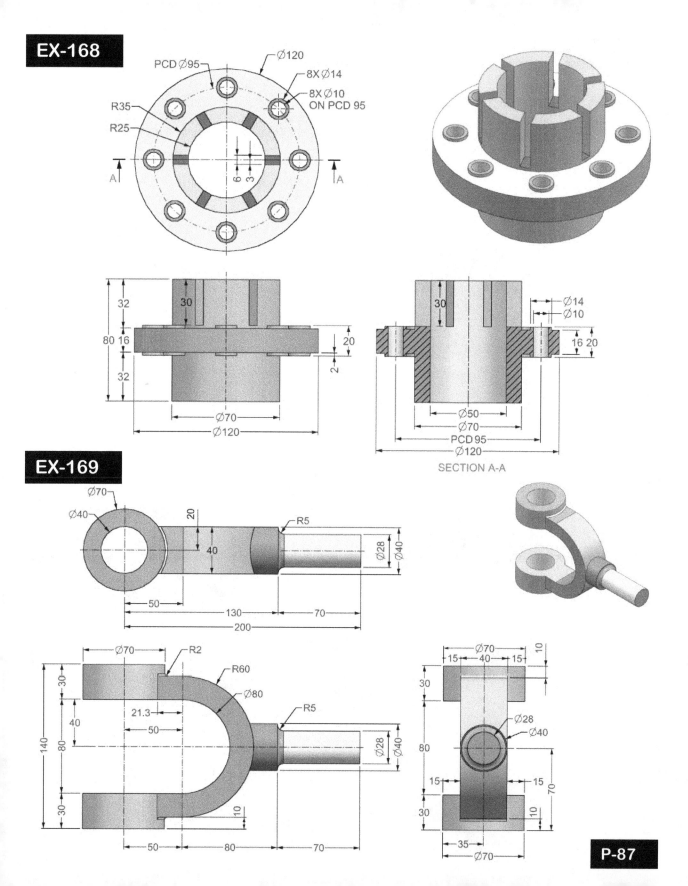

EX-168

PCD Ø95
Ø120
8X Ø14
8X Ø10
ON PCD 95
R35
R25
A A
6 3

32
30
80 16
32
20
2
Ø70
Ø120

30
Ø14
Ø10
16 20
Ø50
Ø70
PCD 95
Ø120

SECTION A-A

EX-169

Ø70
Ø40
20
40
R5
Ø28
Ø40
50
130
70
200

Ø70
R2
R60
Ø80
R5
30
40
21.3
50
80
140
30
Ø28
Ø40
10
50
80
70

Ø70
15 40 15
10
30
Ø28
Ø40
80
15 15
70
30
10
35
Ø70

P-87

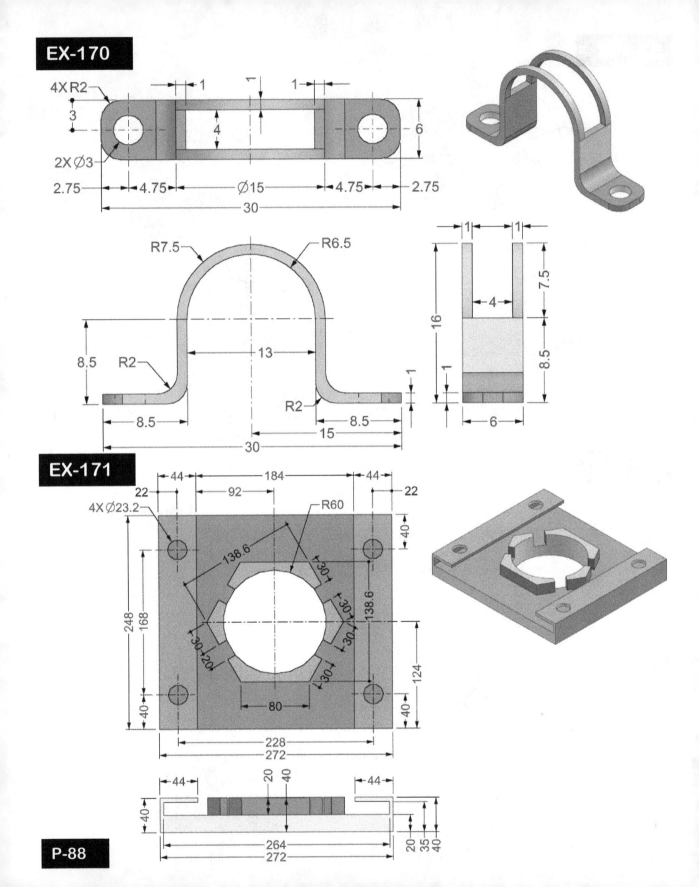

EX-170

4X R2
3
2X ⌀3
2.75
4.75
⌀15
4.75
2.75
30
1
1
1
4
6

R7.5
R6.5
R2
8.5
13
8.5
8.5
15
R2
30
1

1
1
16
7.5
4
8.5
1
6

EX-171

44
184
44
22
92
22
4X ⌀23.2
R60
138.6
30
30
40
138.6
248
168
30
30
20
30
124
30
40
80
40
228
272

44
20
40
44
40
264
272
20
35
40

P-88

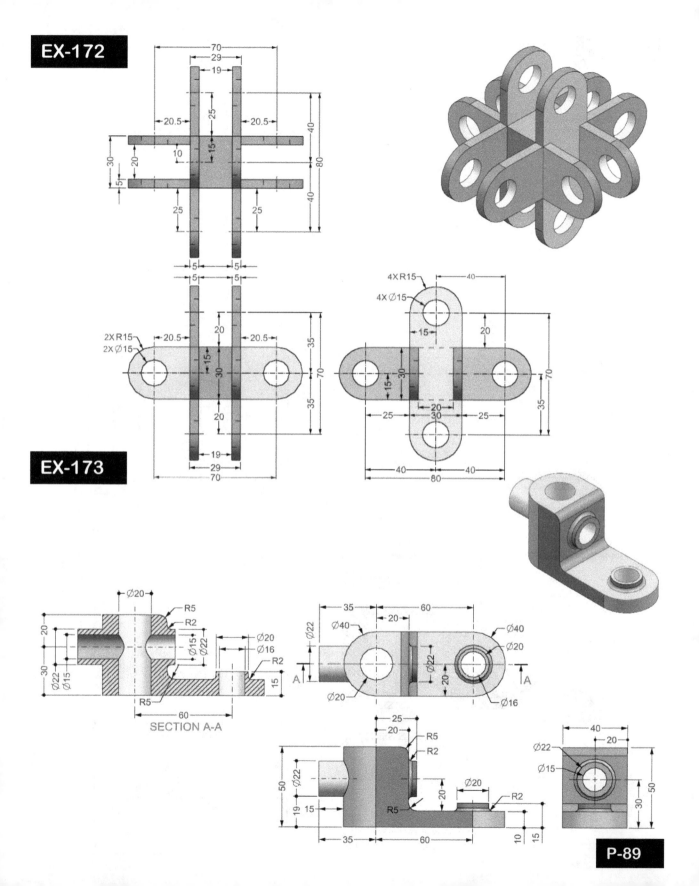

EX-172

EX-173

SECTION A-A

P-89

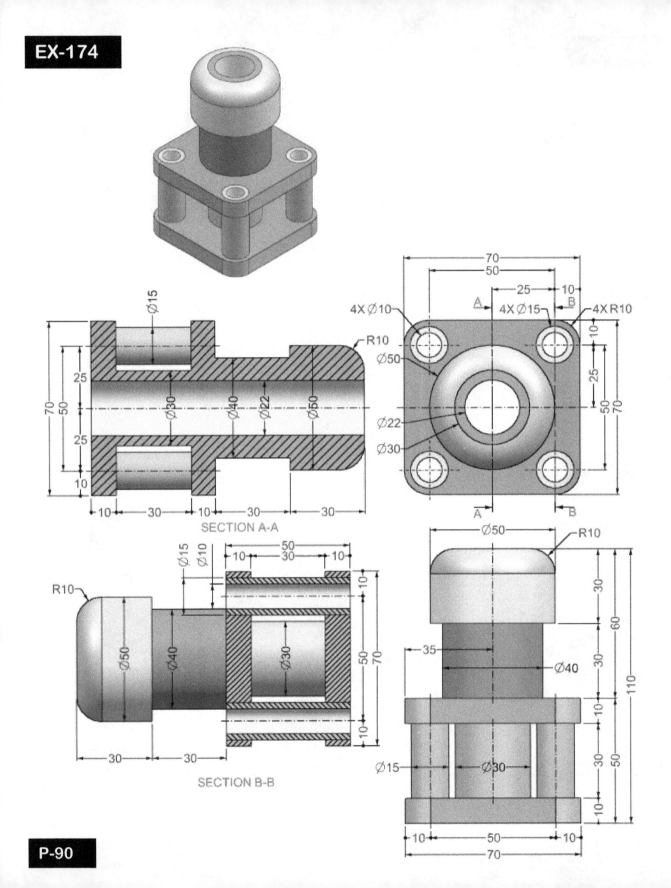

EX-174

SECTION A-A

SECTION B-B

P-90

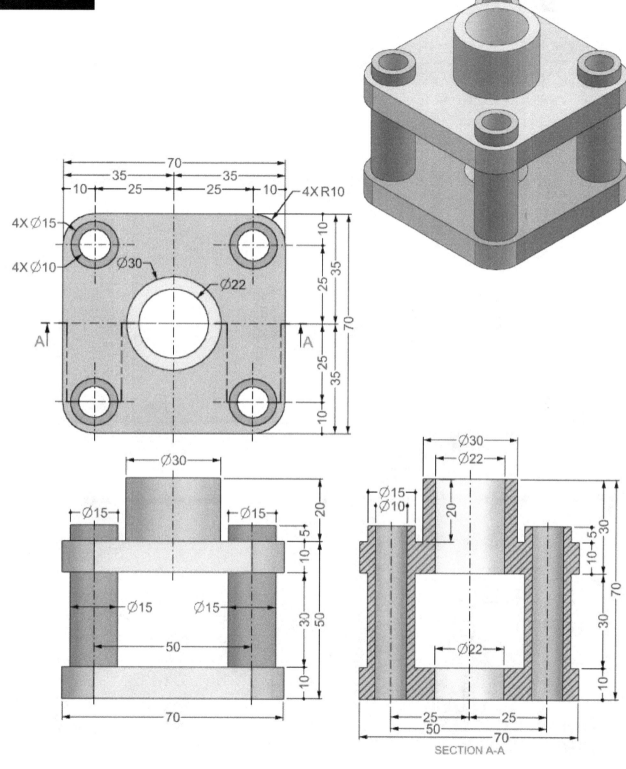

4X Ø15
4X Ø10
Ø30
Ø22
4X R10
70
35
35
10
25
25
10
10
35
25
70
25
35
10

A
A

Ø30
Ø15
Ø15
Ø15
Ø15
50
70
20
5
10
30
50
10

Ø30
Ø22
Ø15
Ø10
Ø22
20
5
10
30
30
70
10
25
25
50
70
SECTION A-A

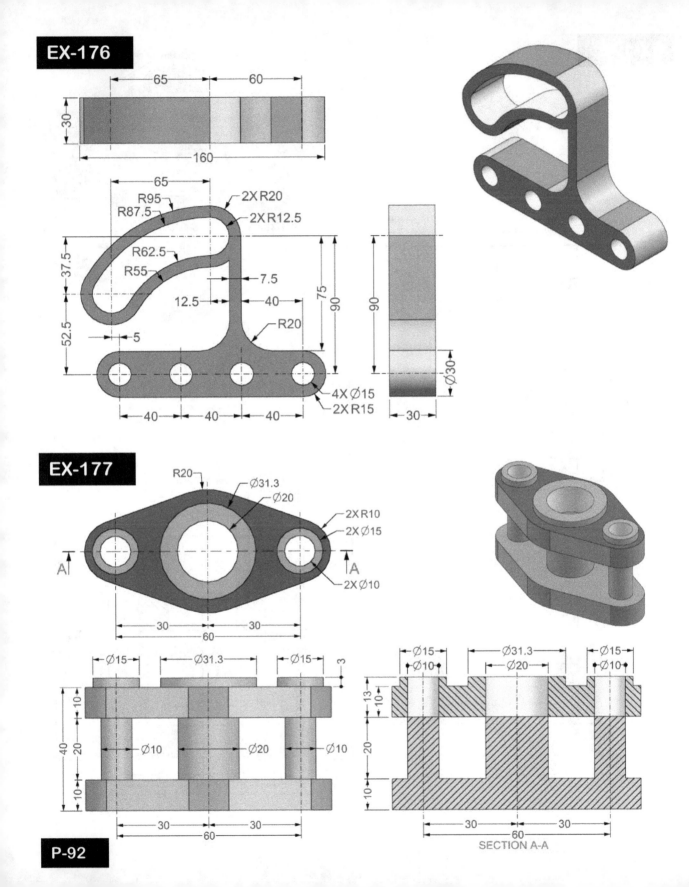

EX-176

65 · 60
30
160

65
R95
R87.5
R62.5
R55
2X R20
2X R12.5
7.5
12.5 · 40
75
90
R20
37.5
52.5
5
90
Ø30
30
40 · 40 · 40
4X Ø15
2X R15

EX-177

R20
Ø31.3
Ø20
2X R10
2X Ø15
2X Ø10
A · A
30 · 30
60

Ø15 · Ø31.3 · Ø15
3
40 · 10 · 20 · 10
Ø10 · Ø20 · Ø10
30 · 30
60

Ø15 · Ø31.3 · Ø15
Ø10 · Ø20 · Ø10
13 · 10
20
10
30 · 30
60
SECTION A-A

P-92

EX-178

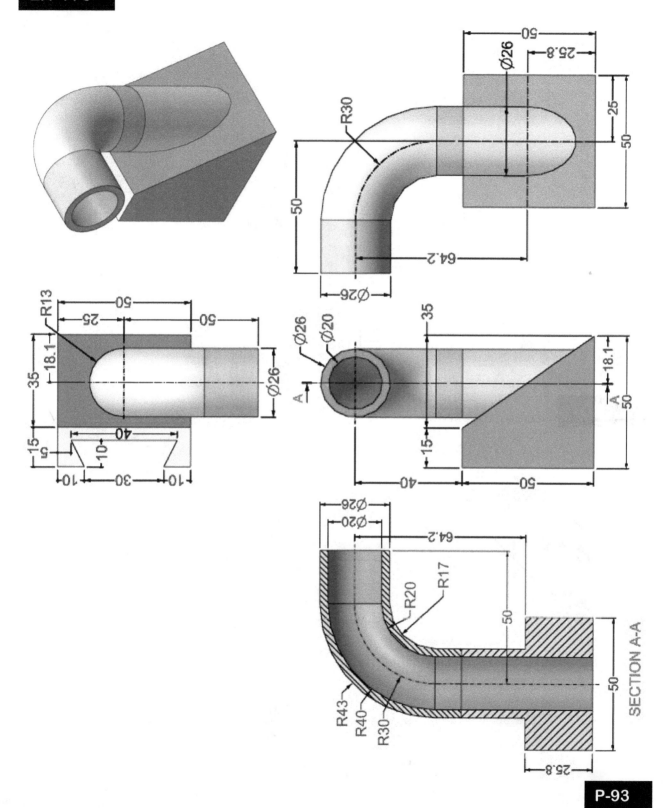

R30
Ø26
50
25.8
25
50
64.2
Ø26

R13
50
25
50
35
18.1
Ø26
15
5
40
10
10
30
10

Ø26
Ø20
35
A
15
40
A
18.1
50
50

Ø26
Ø20
64.2
R20
R17
50
R43
R40
R30
25.8
SECTION A-A

P-93

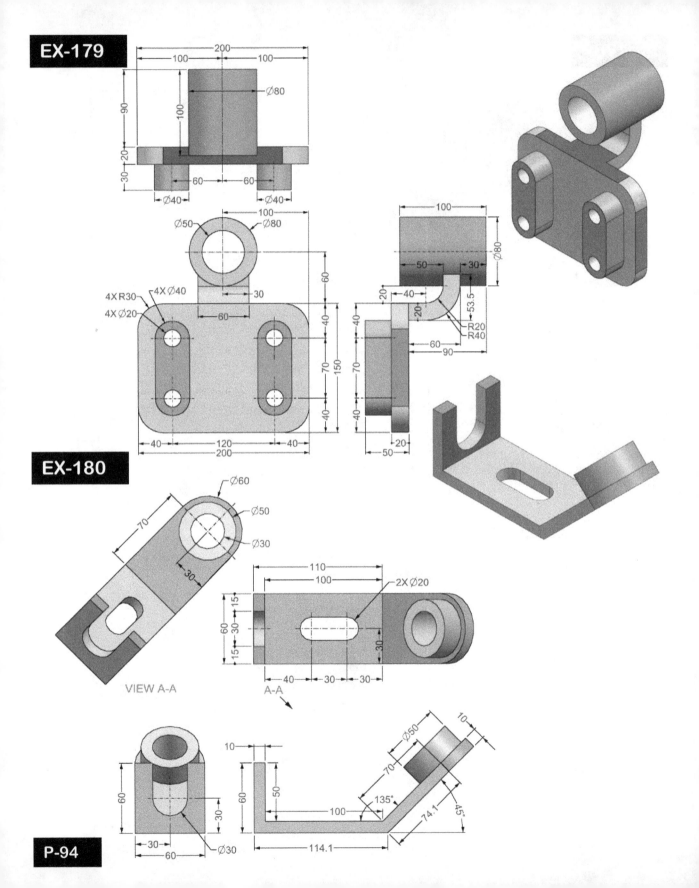

EX-179

EX-180

VIEW A-A

A-A

P-94

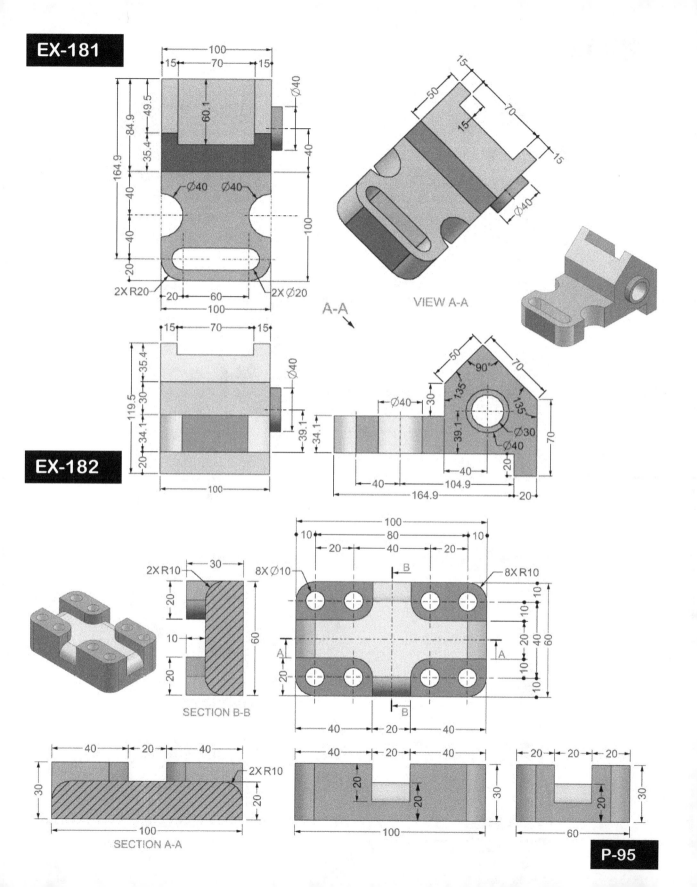

EX-181

EX-182

VIEW A-A

A-A

∅40

∅40   ∅40

2X R20   2X ∅20

∅40

∅40

90°

135   135

∅30
∅40

2X R10   30

8X ∅10   8X R10

SECTION B-B

B

A   A

B

SECTION A-A

2X R10

P-95

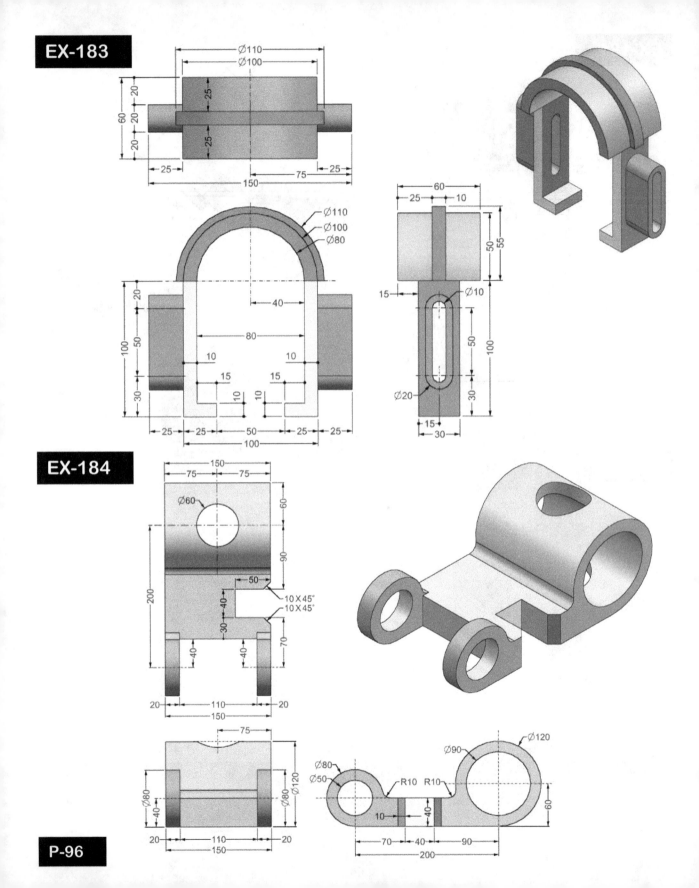

EX-183

⌀110
⌀100
60 / 20 / 20 / 20
25 / 25
⌀110
⌀100
⌀80
25 / 150 / 75 / 25

20 / 100 / 50 / 30
40
80
10 / 10
15 / 15
10 / 10
25 / 25 / 50 / 25 / 25
100

60
25 / 10
50 / 55
15
⌀10
50 / 100
⌀20
15 / 30
30

EX-184

150
75 / 75
⌀60
60
90
200
50
40
10 X 45°
30
10 X 45°
70
40 / 40
20 / 110 / 20
150

75
⌀80
⌀120
⌀80
40
20 / 110 / 20
150

⌀80
⌀50
⌀120
⌀90
R10 R10
10
40
70 / 40 / 90
60
200

P-96

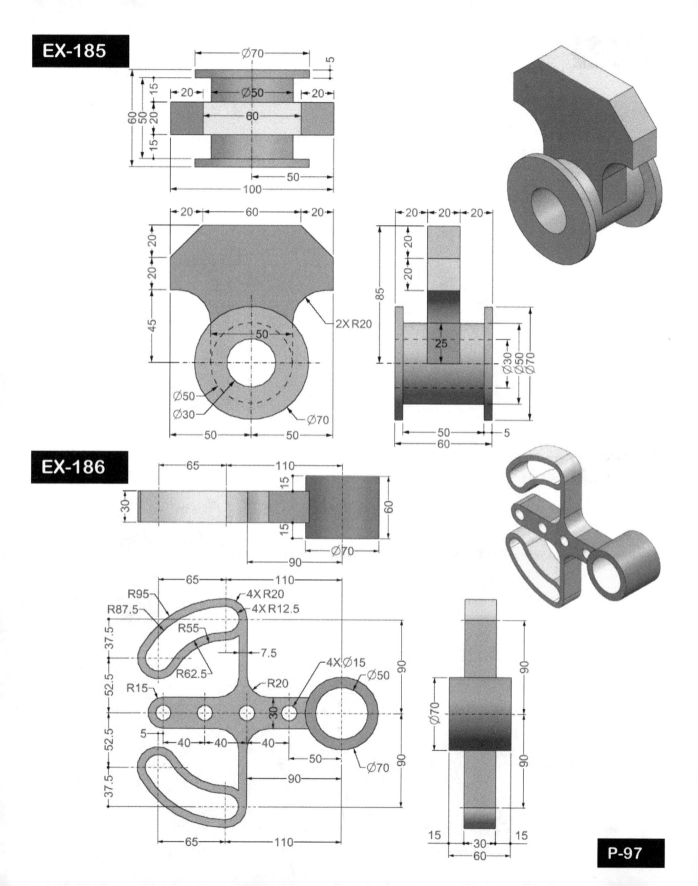

EX-185

Ø70
5
15
20
20
∅50
60
50
20
60
15
20
50
100

20
60
20
20
20
85
45
20
20
20
25
2X R20
∅30
∅50
∅70
50
∅50
∅30
∅70
50
50
50
5
60

EX-186

65
110
30
15
60
15
∅70
90

65
110
R95
4X R20
R87.5
4X R12.5
R55
7.5
37.5
4X∅15
52.5
R62.5
R20
∅50
R15
30
∅70
90
5
90
40
40
40
52.5
50
37.5
90
∅70
65
110

∅70
90
90
15
15
30
60

P-97

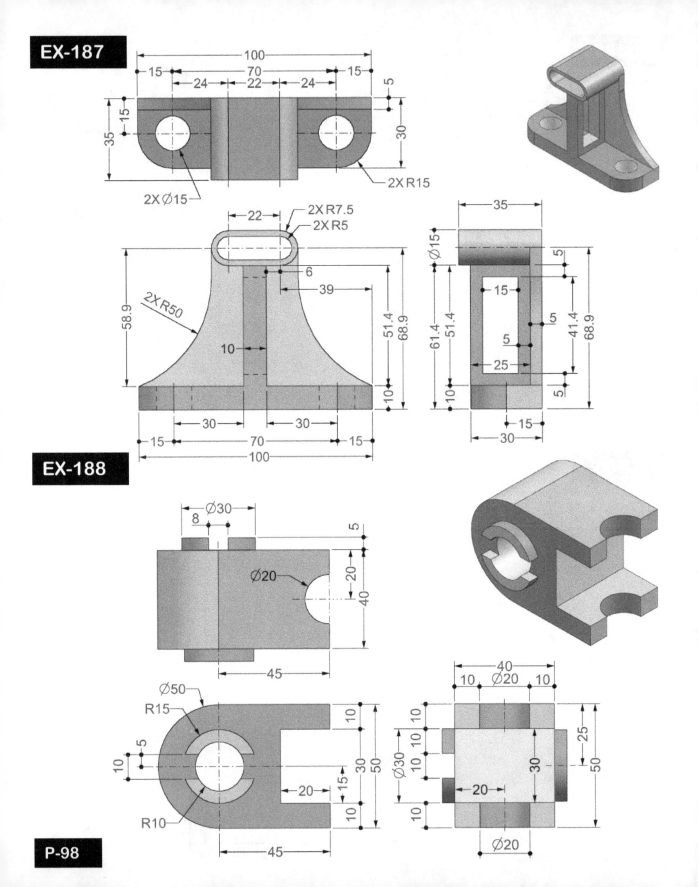

EX-187

100
15 70 15
24 22 24
5
15
35 30
2X R15
2X Ø15

2X R7.5
22 2X R5
6
39
58.9 2X R50 51.4 68.9
10
10
30 30
15 70 15
100

35
Ø15 5
15
5
61.4 51.4 5 41.4 68.9
5
25
10
5
15
30

EX-188

Ø30
8
5
Ø20
20 40
45

Ø50
R15
10 10
5 10 10
10 10
Ø30 30 50 25 30 50
15
20 10 20
R10 10
45 Ø20

40
10 Ø20 10

P-98

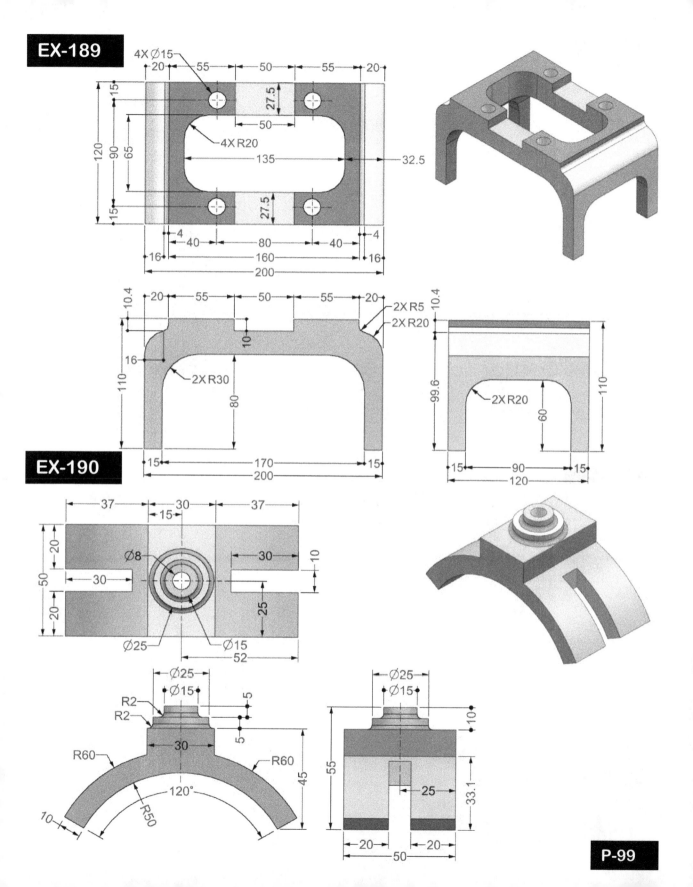

EX-189

EX-190

P-99

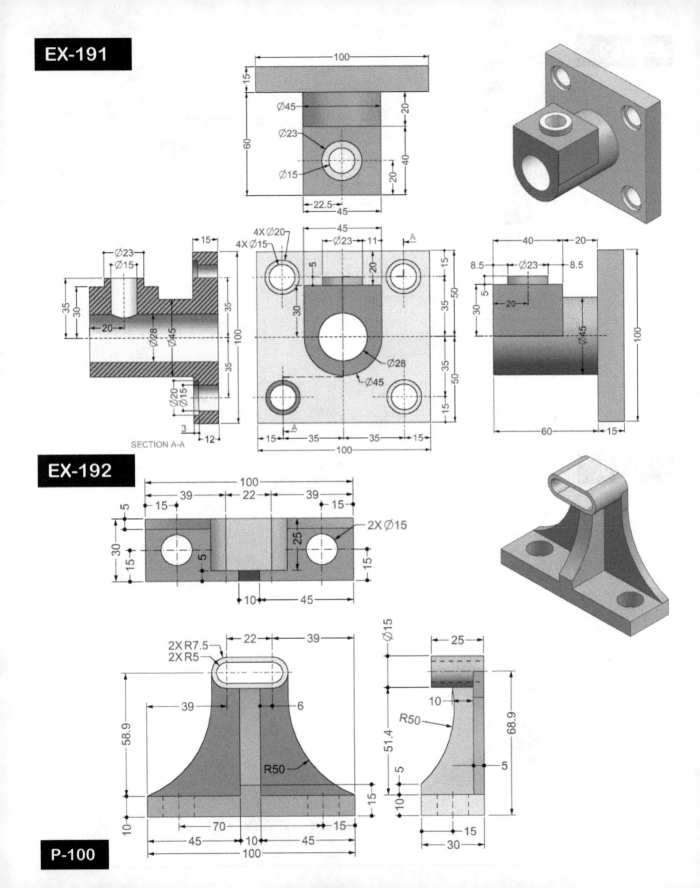

EX-191

EX-192

P-100

EX-193

SECTION A-A

40
12
10
10
80
60
R2
∅20
∅30
1 x 45°
30
10
∅8
∅14

2X R10
2X ∅14
2X ∅8
R20
A
∅30
15
40
30
60
30
10
∅20
∅30
55
A

∅30
∅23
R2
R2
15
55
12
∅14
40
10

40
∅30
∅14
20
R3.2
15
30
30
60
40
10
12

EX-194

4X ∅20
150
110
55
20
20
20
40
40
R5
15
15
130
30
∅120
60
40
30
40
70
35
40

130°
ALL HOLES CHAMFER 2MM
2X ∅20
2X ∅50
25°
∅120
R5
PCD ∅160
∅100
75
80
R5
40
R5
40
70
35
40
20

60
30
15
80
30
40
80
20
R5
40
130

70
50
60
4X ∅20
20
20
110
150
BOTTOM VIEW

P-101

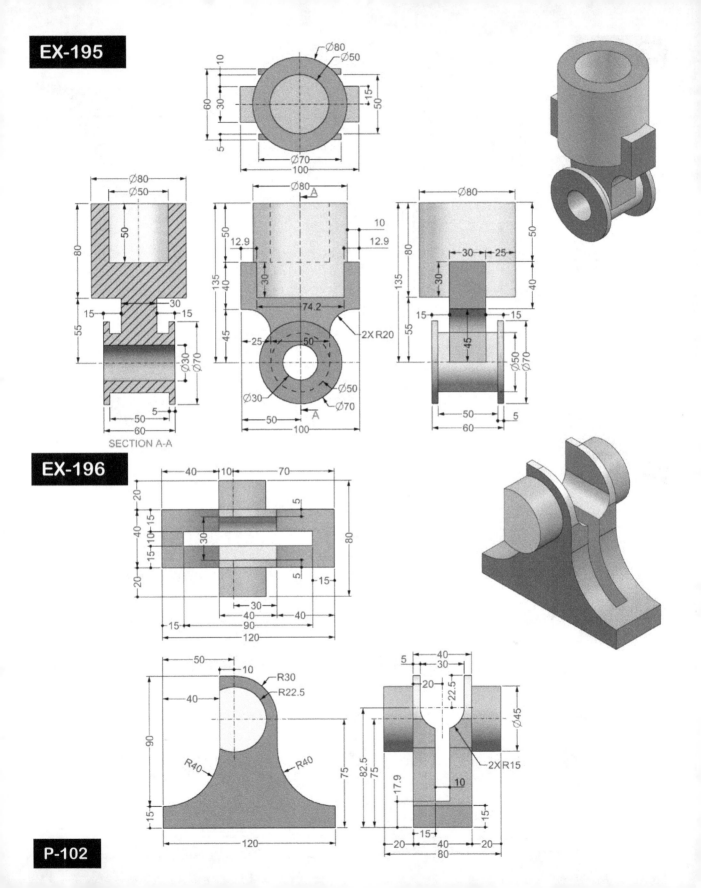

EX-195

Ø80
Ø50
10
60
30
50
15
5
Ø70
100

Ø80
Ø50
80
50
15
30
15
Ø30
Ø70
5
50
60
SECTION A-A

Ø80
A
10
12.9
50
12.9
135
40
30
74.2
45
2X R20
25
50
Ø30
Ø50
Ø70
50
100
A

Ø80
50
80
30
25
135
30
55
15
15
45
Ø50
Ø70
50
5
60

EX-196

40
10
70
20
5
40
15
10
30
80
15
5
15
30
40
40
15
90
120

50
10
R30
R22.5
40
90
R40
R40
75
15
120

5
40
30
20
22.5
82.5
75
Ø45
17.9
2X R15
10
15
20
40
20
80
15

P-102

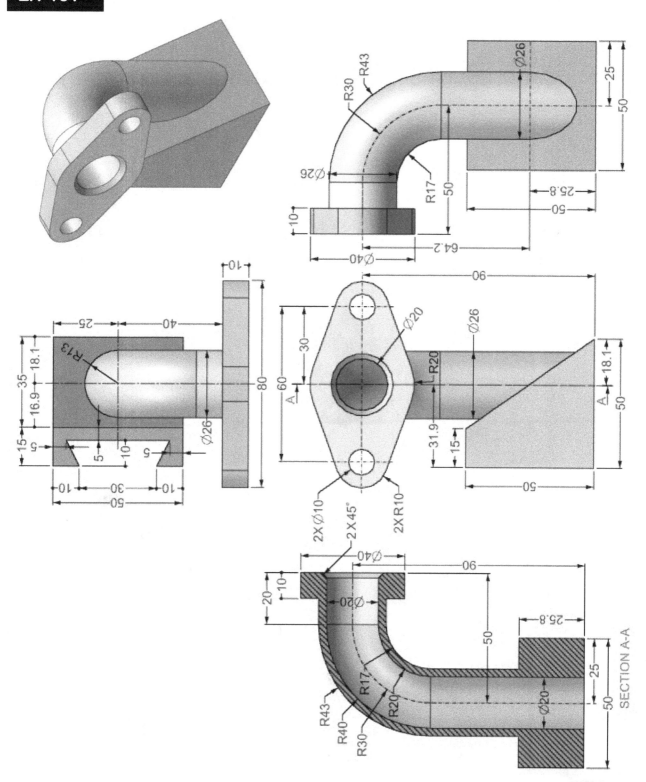

Ø26
R43
R30
25
50
Ø26
R17
50
25.8
50
10
64.2
Ø40

10
25
40
R13
35
18.1
16.9
15
5
Ø26
5
10
5
10
30
10
50
80

90
Ø20
30
60
A
Ø26
R20
A
18.1
31.9
50
15
50
2X Ø10
2 X 45°
2X R10

Ø40
20
10
Ø20
90
25.8
R17
50
25
R43
R20
Ø20
50
R40
R30
SECTION A-A

6X Ø15 THRU
ON PCD 90
Ø120
Ø50
Ø40

PCD Ø90

Ø120
Ø50
Ø40
15
10
Ø15
120
30

5
10
60°
60°
Ø20
Ø30
PCD 54
80
Ø10

SECTION A-A

B-B

VIEW B-B

Ø20

8X Ø10 THRU
ON PCD 54
Ø30
Ø70
PCD Ø54

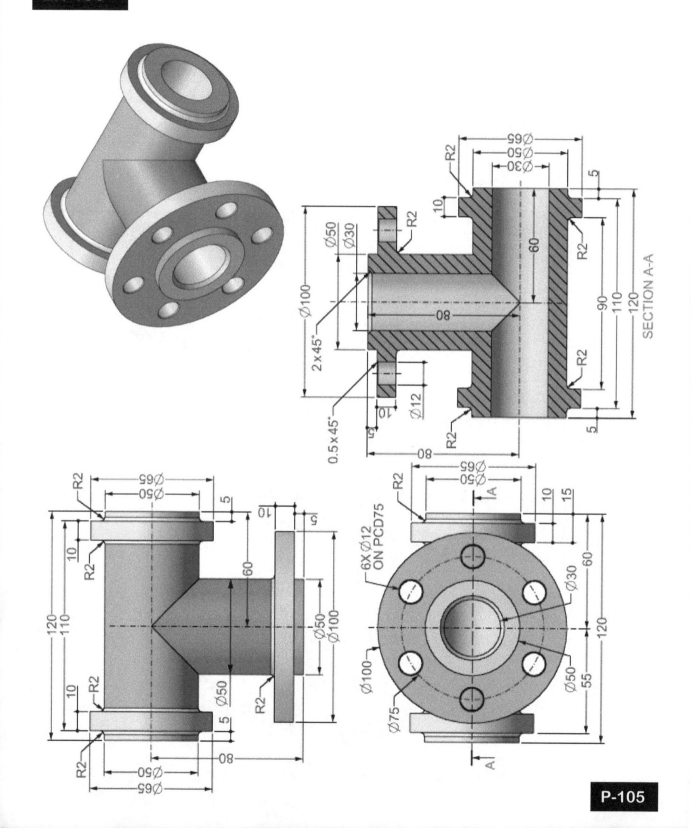

SECTION A-A

Ø65
Ø50
Ø30
R2
10
60
R2
90
110
120
5
R2
R2
5

Ø100
Ø50
Ø30
R2
80
2×45°
0.5×45°
Ø12
10
5
R2
80

R2
Ø65
Ø50
5
10
5
60
120
110
10
R2
80
Ø50
Ø65
R2
Ø50
Ø100
R2
R2

R2
Ø65
Ø50
6X Ø12
ON PCD75
A
10
15
Ø30
60
120
55
Ø50
Ø100
Ø75
A

∅90
∅76

SECTION C-C

∅86
∅34
D-D

2XR10

DETAIL D-D
SCALE 2:1

∅24
12
10
∅20

Thickness 2 mm
All sides

SECTION B-B

33
12
84
∅34
2
17
3X45°
∅30

B
20
60
45
22
∅80
∅90
C
C
B

R5
∅90
∅80
102
2

∅90
∅30
∅80
A
A

3X45°
R5
R3
∅80
∅76
17
∅30
∅84

Thickness 2 mm
All sides

∅86
∅90
102

SECTION A-A

Other useful books by CADIN360

1. 150 CAD Exercises

2. AutoCAD Exercises

3. CAD Exercises

4. 50+ SolidWorks Exercises

5. SolidWorks 200 Exercises

6. Autodesk Inventor Exercises

7. Catia Exercises

8. Siemens NX Exercises